THOUGHTS OF A TEENAGER

REFLECTIONS OF A BOY BECOMING A MAN

AJAYNATH R

Copyright © Ajaynath R
All Rights Reserved.

This book has been self-published with all reasonable efforts taken to make the material error-free by the author. No part of this book shall be used, reproduced in any manner whatsoever without written permission from the author, except in the case of brief quotations embodied in critical articles and reviews.

The Author of this book is solely responsible and liable for its content including but not limited to the views, representations, descriptions, statements, information, opinions and references ["Content"]. The Content of this book shall not constitute or be construed or deemed to reflect the opinion or expression of the Publisher or Editor. Neither the Publisher nor Editor endorse or approve the Content of this book or guarantee the reliability, accuracy or completeness of the Content published herein and do not make any representations or warranties of any kind, express or implied, including but not limited to the implied warranties of merchantability, fitness for a particular purpose. The Publisher and Editor shall not be liable whatsoever for any errors, omissions, whether such errors or omissions result from negligence, accident, or any other cause or claims for loss or damages of any kind, including without limitation, indirect or consequential loss or damage arising out of use, inability to use, or about the reliability, accuracy or sufficiency of the information contained in this book.

Made with ♥ on the Notion Press Platform
www.notionpress.com

> *"Thank you for all the pain that made me alone for a while and woke the thinker in me."*

Contents

Foreword — xiii

Acknowledgements — xv

Prologue — xvii

1. Passion — 1
2. A Worst Habit — 2
3. Masculinity — 4
4. The Marshmallow Test — 5
5. PTSD — 7
6. Perfectionism Is A Crime — 8
7. The Compound Effect — 9
8. Isolation : Boon Or Bane — 11
9. Modern Music Is Worser Than You Thought...! — 13
10. Ego Is The Enemy...! — 14
11. Hurry Or Hustle...? — 16
12. Art Of Endurance — 17
13. Follow The Trend! — 19
14. 6000 Attempts — 20
15. Happiness Is A Pracatice — 21
16. Karna My Fav — 22
17. Social Media Justice..! — 23
18. The 0.001% Group — 24
19. Theory Of Comparison — 25
20. The 3D Experience — 26
21. The Best Reward Is The Work Iteslf — 27

Contents

22. The Identity Effect		29
23. Cheat Code For No Fap...!!!		30
24. Theory Of Introverts		31
25. The Sigma Male		33
26. Being INFJ		34
27. 3 Types Of Men		35
28. Truth About Exams		36
29. Just Dive In		38
30. Modern Wisdom		39
31. The Modern Problem		41
32. The Private Space		42
33. Credit Takers		43
34. Being A Nice Guy		44
35. How To Remove Bad Habits		45
36. The NEET Scam		47
37. 50% GOD Thoerem		48
38. The Social Media...!		49
39. Read More...		51
40. Feel Your Feelings		52
41. Career...!		53
42. Power Of Now!!		54
43. Let's Talk About Women!!		55
44. Choosing The Right Pain		57
45. Brainwashed Cult		59

Contents

46. Life Of An Eagle	60
47. The Batman	62
48. How To Read A Book	64
49. The Spotlight Effect	65
50. Diet	67
51. Monk Mode	68
52. The Gen Z	70
53. The Gagan Boys	72
54. Listeners	74
55. Learn A New Skill	76
56. How To Learn A Language	77
57. Moderate Speed	79
58. Learn To Limit	80
59. Decisions	81
60. Understanding Sleep: The Difference Between Bedtime And Sleep Time	82
61. Lessons From Dear Zindagi	84
62. The Circumstances	85
63. Anybody Can Fake Their Own Character	87
64. Warning...!	89
65. The Most Valuable Thing Isn't Time; It Is Attention	91
66. Harder Things....	93
67. The Spider-Man	94

Contents

68. Don't Burn Your Engine...!	96
69. Friendship	98
70. Where To Find Your Wife...?	100
71. Make Texting Your Last Priority	102
72. Keeping The Consistency	104
73. Out Work Them All	106
74. Happens Over Time.....	108
75. Dear INFJ Me....	109
76. Modern Dating	113
77. Stop Being A Nerd	114
78. Live Your Truth	116
79. The Enemies	118
80. Action And Intention	120
81. Necessity...	121
82. Happiness For Sale	123
83. Stoicism And Ryan Holiday	125
84. How To Win In Public Speaking	127
85. Stress And Pressure..	129
86. The Chad	131
87. Gurudwara	132
88. How To Groom Well	134
89. Clean Them Up...	136
90. Fix Your Roots	137
91. Fake Your Feelings	138

Contents

92. Power Of Authenticity	139
93. Go For Engineering Babe...	140
94. #Truth	141
95. How To Sleep Well	142
96. The Art Of Saying No	144
97. Screen Time	145
98. Be A Stoic	147
99. Don't Miss 2 Days...	148
100. Expectations	149
101. Fear...	150
102. Bulk In Results	152
103. Signs Of Poor Mental Health	153
104. Brain Health Vs Mental Health	154
105. Truths About The Rich	156
106. Dear Providers	157
107. Features	159
108. Art Of Staying Hard	160
109. Beware This Madness	161
110. Keep Some Boundaries	163
111. Stop This Bullshit	165
After Word	167
Tink Talks	169
My Reading List	171
About The Author	177

"Great people always talk about great things, right? But what if a random person started speaking profound truths? That means they must have witnessed something great...
"

Sharing some feedback from readers—the real fuel behind this drive:

"Actually, this felt really good for me. The whole progression and the little things you mentioned made for a wonderful experience"
~ Asreya

"After reading it, I realized it's not just about a boy transitioning into manhood"
~"it is very connected to real life, and it helps me to make new habits."
~ Gowri

"It changed my perspective and made me chuckle a couple of times here and there when i came to know that there are ppl out there making the mistakes that i did"
~Desh

"A great start to a promising writing journeyit is a journey through growth and self discovery of any teenagers life."
~ Kavya
"One of the strengths of the book lies in its relatability.Teenagers, as well as adults who have lived through these years, will recognize elements of themselves within the pages"
~ Nasar Anwar
"I love how u show ur real life examples and try to relate to the subject"
~ Abhijith

Foreword

What if the answers I'm searching for are hidden in my own questions? In this book, I share a raw, unfiltered look into my journey of self-discovery through personal journaling. Filled with doubts, questions, and deep reflections, each page reveals an intimate conversation with myself—an exploration of pain, healing, and the search for meaning.

As I wrestle with my own thoughts, I uncover insights that guide me through trauma, leading me toward resilience and clarity. This collection of journal entries isn't about having all the answers; it's about embracing the uncertainty and discovering strength in self-reflection.

For anyone navigating life's challenges, this book offers a relatable glimpse into my inner journey and serves as a reminder that healing often starts from within.

~Ajaynath R

Acknowledgements

First, I would like to thank my friends Abhinand, Achyuth, Riyas and Alok for being there during my worst days and helping me to rise.

I must also thank my beloved teachers, Madhumohan Sir, Vinod Sir, Lissy Teacher, and Usha Teacher, for supporting me at every stage of my life.

I express my gratitude to the cover designer, Adarsh, who has been my creative partner since my college days.

A book like this required extensive editing and formatting, and the contributions of my editors, Riyas and Haridev, were truly admirable.

My parents, Sajitha Ramanathan and Ramanathan, and my brother, Amalnath, deserve endless thanks for their love and support.

I also express my gratitude to the viewers of Tink Talks, who were the true inspiration to publish this book.

Finally, this book is a reminder to myself that, while I may fail, I am not a failure. I want to thank myself for never giving up on life.

~ Ajaynath R

Prologue

During my 6th grade, my father asked me to read the Bhagavad Gita daily. At that age, I had no real interest in reading, so I struggled to start. I managed to reach the third chapter, but I felt nothing—I was too immature to understand any of it. So, I stopped reading.

Reading became my favorite habit in 2022. The first book I read was Wings of Fire by Dr. APJ Abdul Kalam. From there, I moved on to books by Robin Sharma, Ryan Holiday, and various philosophers, including Mark Manson. Between these two phases, I went through a period of pain.

I was deeply bullied—not during school, but in college in my twenties. Betrayal from my coworkers and friends put me into a state of distrust. A series of events, like a breakup, back-to-back injuries, hospital stays, political issues around my extracurricular activities, and typical college drama, led to severe trauma. I struggled to focus on my studies, lost contact with friends, and failed to show respect for my teachers. I believed the world was a nasty place. I even lost trust in my parents, a choice I regretted a few years later. The anger, pain, and frustration drove me into deep isolation. That's when I turned to books.

I realized I was behaving poorly with friends, teachers, and even family members. Isolation became my only relief. I began practicing karate, meditating, journaling, and reading—a total self-improvement journey.

Years later, I continued this path even after leaving those traumatic, isolated days behind. This helped me rebuild myself. In 2024, I read the Gita three times, which surprised my parents. I started gaining weight by hitting the gym, became a consistent meditator, and I realized I was

PROLOGUE

far ahead of my former self. Throughout this journey, the habits of reading, journaling, and solitary reflection led me to write and share some of my thoughts and findings.

This book is a collection of thoughts from my journal—insights gained from books, personal reflections, and doubts. It's not a self-help guide, just a journey from being a lonely boy to becoming a man.

This book arises from the thoughts and insights I gained during my darkest days. It is not a guide or a self-help book but rather the reflections of a boy who suffered deeply and emerged as a man.

Here, I share some essential tools that brought me freedom, happiness, and fulfillment. Dear readers, I invite all of you to join me on a journey of self-discovery.

CHAPTER ONE

PASSION

The most overrated word of this era!!.
Social media is governed by passion junkies who have no idea what it means. and i had one....
But, the illusion of passion weakened me!
So, were the giants who made it fake? Nah.. But it was their Purpose!
Tom Cruise, the man who accomplishes incredible stunts without fail even in his fifties, considers it his mission to entertain others. Cristiano Ronaldo, even in his fourties, maintains his body like a bull, why? Football is more than simply a pastime for him;
When I discovered something intriguing that I thought was my passion, I began working hard to fulfill my so-called passion, which made me nervous and greedy. Rather than focusing on the process, I was more interested in the results, which caused me to become worried and alienated from my friends and family, and I finally lost a little piece of myself
Are you motivated by your passion or your purpose?
If it is purpose, then there is a magical word for your life which is
IKIGAI.

CHAPTER TWO

A Worst Habit

The worst habit of Malayalees all over the world is to have the worst morning breakfast!!! full of sugar, oil, and even baked items .We rise just brush and get into the most unhealthy morning routine..

For the past 22 years I was also the same...!

But.. imagine we were living in the stone age! We wake up early then there won't be anything to eat, we have to go hunting or climb a tree for food. Maybe it will take hours to get our first hand of food. In simple words we fast for hours, by that time we engage in some physical activities, we have our morning sunlight, we engage in group tasks and finally we get our food.

So that the cavemen were more productive than us, they were more masculine, strong and had high testosterone levels too.

But today most of us just grab our phones and start scrolling early in the morning...!.

Neither have a morning routine nor are they interested in fasting.

Just go for a run, read a few pages, meditate for 5 minutes and take a cold shower too. Then have some clean food which is free from sugar, Oil and all those junk items.

just a clean breakfast!!!
lte me explain my moring routine
And finally let me ask you one thing.
Do you have the courage to fast for at least 2 hours in the morning?

CHAPTER THREE

MASCULINITY

Andrew Tate..will be the one who introduced this to the Gen z...

Many of us began to know about the term masculinity by this red pill guy.

Just out of curiosity I started searching for the meaning of masculinity. Is it real? Or just a toxic concept made by these red pill guys ?

Finally ended with a book named "The way of the superior man " by David Deida. And here is what I learned from it.

For a Masculine man It is not about getting into a fight, just staying calm in every situation.

Not mating with as many women, just raising a good family.

Hanging out and having fun?? Naah... having a clear mission and purpose in his life!!!!

The one who takes care of his family, business and health. He is hardworking, helping, humble and well disciplined. So do the red pill guys have these traits or do the legends like Nicola Tesla, Mahatma Gandhi and Martin Luther King were the true masculine figures?

CHAPTER FOUR

The Marshmallow Test

The marsh mellow test was developed by psychologist Walter Mischel in the late 1960s and early 1970s, involves giving a child a treat and offering a choice: eat it immediately or wait about 15 minutes to receive a second treat. The test explores delayed gratification and its correlation with future success and self-control. Follow-up studies found that children who waited tended to have better outcomes in areas like academic performance, health, and overall well-being.

Yeah, delayed gratification matters..

The Marshmallow test proved the positive side of delayed gratification. But it is hard to remove the opposite Which is Instant gratification! Which causes mental retardation and fatigue...

1. Grabbing the phone at each and every minute even there is nothing for you
2. Eating the sweets even after a full stomach

3. Sleeping for less than 5 hours or more than 10 hours
4. Watching porn and Swimming in the social media
Well there is no need for a question ,because we know in which category we belong to!

CHAPTER FIVE

PTSD

" What doesn't kill you makes you stronger" suggests that adversity leads to personal growth
Does that really happen?
Imagine a youngster who experienced any of them throughout his early years, such as bullying, sexual assault, domestic violence, or any other tragedy.
Do they act as though they've never experienced it? definitely Not ..!!
They struggle with their studies, friendships, and careers.
It's known as trauma in a nutshell. Those who have experienced it are suffering from post-traumatic stress disorder (PTSD). which has an impact on their mental health.
The hippocampus and amygdala exhibit altered neuronal activity. can also cause melancholy, worry, fear, and impaired memory.
If they never recover from it formally That will be detrimental to their emotional well-being. Perhaps, "What doesn't kill you, makes you a stranger.": Joker (The Dark Knight)

CHAPTER SIX

PERFECTIONISM IS A CRIME

There is a story of two young men who decided to get in shape. Both of them decided to join a gym. The first one joined a fitness club near his house the very next day.

The second one spent one week searching for the best gym in his locality. He spent some days learning about the best diet to follow. He researched the best workout routines, the best exercises, and so on...

Three months passed. The first one who just joined a gym learned the best diet from his trainer after hitting a rep. He made his own workout routine by examining his colleagues there. He learned the best time to grind, and as a result, he started bulking up.

But the second one, who was a perfectionist, waited for the perfect time, space, and conditions to start. In reality, they never existed at all.

Perfection is a fantasy; it detaches us from reality. Just put your ass on the line, and things will happen.

Start working on the project that you have postponed for weeks, and start doing the tasks assigned to you.

Because the hardest thing is always to get started..

CHAPTER SEVEN

The Compound Effect

If you improve by 1% each day, the rate is 0.01, and the number of periods is 365 (for a year).

$$(1+0.01)^{365} \approx 37.78$$

This means that a 1% daily improvement compounds to approximately 37.78 times better over the course of a year, showing the power of consistency.

What about the opposite? If you decrease by 1% each day,

$$(1-0.01)^{365} \approx 0.03$$

This means that reducing by 1% each day would result in being approximately 0.03 times, or 3% of what you started with, after one year. This highlights the importance of avoiding small, consistent declines over time.

Here comes the concept of the compound effect.

We often start something big and end up with absolutely nothing because we weren't consistent!

But what if we started with a tiny step, just 1%, but each day it makes huge progress?

Going to the gym every day, reading a page every day, meditating for 5 minutes every day matters…!

And the truth is consistency defines whether it is going to be better or bitter!
~Credits: Atomic Habits.

CHAPTER EIGHT

ISOLATION : BOON OR BANE

Does detaching from others have a positive impact, or is it always negative?

Let's consider two situations. The first one involves spending your alone time with junk habits like Netflix, video games, or any other non-productive activities.

The second one is when you commit yourself to a specific task or assignment. You retreat into a cold and dark space, using your full attention to achieve that particular goal.

Yes, the second one will feel more pleasurable than the first. Why? Because of the flow state.

For some people, isolation may not be a threat to their daily life. They socialize only to recharge their soul. Many productivity gurus have mentioned the method of "monk mode" over the past few decades, where isolation is the root of their productivity.

Actually, it depends on how we use it.

But nobody advises lifelong isolation, so being alone for a while can be interesting if you are productive with your routine.

THOUGHTS OF A TEENAGER

In fact, how we deal with isolation matters the most.

CHAPTER NINE

Modern Music Is Worser Than You Thought…!

I was a big fan of rap and pop music. Eminem and XXXTentacion ruled my playlist during my teenage years. The rhythm and beats fried my brain… But then I realized the lyrics that I was consuming literally ruined my thoughts, because they were full of the following words: F*ck, Pu**y, B*ich. And I was consuming it for years!

I was consistently listening to dirty and disgusting music only because of the dopamine it created in my mind. Well, rappers are now making a huge base in Malayalam songs, and unparliamentary words are common. We support it as a trend, but we have no idea how much it spoils our minds… During the 90s and early 2000s, songs were meaningful, and there were so many poetic aspects to each and every song.

But today, it is exactly the opposite. Well, it is always our choice to listen to what we like.But remember, we become what we consume…

CHAPTER TEN

EGO IS THE ENEMY...!

According to Ryan Holiday, the American population consists of a large number of people who are often referred to as "bitches" and "bastards."

Here's why: after a breakup, Americans have a tendency to blame the other person, calling them a "bastard" or a "bitch." This terminology is prevalent in the USA.

Why is this the case? When we experience pain from a beloved person, group, or place, it tears us apart. We suffer greatly and struggle to accept the situation, leading us to hate.

We use hate as a coping mechanism. We blame others and create negative stories about them in our minds. However, as a result, we never truly get over it. Even years later, when we revisit that painful moment, we feel the same agony.

We try our best to avoid, blame, and even forget those who hurt us, but it never works because of the lingering hate.

To truly move on, we must accept reality and forgive.

Forgive those circumstances. Forgive those people.
Because forgiveness is love.
It takes a lot of courage to do so.
In fact, forgiveness is not only for others; it is the best thing we can do for ourselves.

CHAPTER ELEVEN

Hurry Or Hustle...?

Imagine you have a task that needs to be completed by 6 PM. It's a bit tough. How do you manage it? Do you postpone all your other work, cut your lunch and free time, hurry, and finish by 5:50?

Or do you stay calm, take 10 minutes to analyze the work, divide it into small steps, discipline yourself for each task, take enough time to rest, and just finish it? In other words, do you hustle?

Hustle is always better than hurrying. Always....!

When we are in a hurry, we make trouble. There is a simple proof in physics: as the velocity increases, so does the entropy.

In order to go faster, we have to go smoothly. To go smoothly, we have to go slow.

As we all know, slow and steady wins the race!

CHAPTER TWELVE

ART OF ENDURANCE

When I was in my karate class, our Sensei asked us to do 50 push-ups as part of our yellow belt test. We started, and by the time we reached 35, we felt a tremendous amount of pain and fatigue. All of us stopped at 42 or 43.

The very next day, we were asked to do the same, but this time our Sensei used a different approach in counting. He counted like this: 1, 2, 3, 4, 5, 6, 7, 8, then reversed the count to 7, 6, 5, 4, 3, and then started counting forward again: 4, 5, 6, 7. We couldn't measure the correct number of push-ups; we just kept repeating our grind. After a while, we felt the same pain as the day before.

Our Sensei then told us to stop. None of us had any idea about the total number of push-ups we did. But when our Sensei, who had been counting on his phone, showed us the result, we were stunned! It was 67 push-ups!

Same people, same task, but the approach was different! It wasn't our bodies that felt fatigue; it was our lazy minds. Yes, it happens. Sometimes our minds chant to our brains that it's enough and we're tired. And we quit.

THOUGHTS OF A TEENAGER

In many cases, our bodies may feel pain, frustration, and fatigue, but it is our minds that control our actions. To move forward in those situations, we have to put a command into our brains:

Not yet!

CHAPTER THIRTEEN

FOLLOW THE TREND!

Angela Merkel was a German politician and also worked as a quantum chemist for years. She wore the exact same type of dress and had the same boxy haircut until her last day. Once, a reporter asked her: "Don't you have anything else?"

She replied: "I'm a Civil servant, not a model."

Well, We Malayalees have the urge to follow trends and have been known for unnecessary purchasing over the past decade. We always stay up to date with trends only for external validation. We buy, wear, and take some cool photos, then wait for the validation of others.

Steve Jobs found a perfect jacket for his comfort and wore the same item for the rest of his life. Similarly, there is another legend named Kalam, who wore the exact same outfit throughout his journey, during meetings, site visits, and conferences.

The trend always changes every 5-7 months, and we spend thousands for it. And the cool photos? Nobody even remembers them. In fact, nobody cares!

CHAPTER FOURTEEN

6000 ATTEMPTS

Edison never admitted himself as brilliant or generous. Here is why...

Once he mentioned that he was just adopting the inventions of others and putting them all together in the right way. Then how did he find the right way?

By practicing...

There were hundreds of scientists who were trying their best to find the best thickness for the tungsten filament for a bulb, but every one of them tried with the same strategy.

But he was the one who tried with a variety of ideas. After 6,000 attempts, he tried with the thickness of a hair and found the best one.

And he remarked: it was simple. How could someone get a different result by using the same method?

CHAPTER FIFTEEN

HAPPINESS IS A PRACATICE

I was brainwashed since my childhood that 10th standard is the life-changing point. So, you have to work hard to get good marks, otherwise...

But after 10th standard, it was +2. The same thing repeated...

Then? Of course, it was graduation. I accomplished Engineering from a prestigious college!

Now go for a job... Build your career... And so on. And the reality is, it is never going to end...

Each and every destination took a tremendous amount of work and commitment. In fact, the top of one mountain was the bottom of another.

And the myth of becoming happy after completing a particular task was a mirage. Life is an endless journey, and among that voyage, the only way to become happy is to choose it.

And it is only possible by gratitude.

Things are going to change; nothing is permanent. The feeling of being grateful for what I have today brings fulfillment.

CHAPTER SIXTEEN

KARNA MY FAV

My favorite character in the Mahabharata was Karna.
He was abandoned by his mother and left his family to learn the art of war. When he came back, nobody accepted him as a warrior; instead, they insulted him as a "Suthaputra"

He was the best on the battlefield. He sacrificed his own "kavach and kundala." He was honest and helpful too. But he failed against Arjuna. Even Lord Krishna cried during his death. Was it bad luck?

In reality, it wasn't bad luck; it was a bad choice. Because he knew he was standing on the wrong side. Blinded by his friendship with Duryodhana, he was also partaking in "Adharma."

Karna already knew the fact that truth and justice (Dharma) would prevail in the end, but he chose the other side.

Yes, choices do matter. Having wisdom, knowledge, and courage are good qualities, but if you are on the wrong side with all these qualities, using them for evil ends, then you may end up like Karna.

It is always the choice, not luck!

CHAPTER SEVENTEEN

SOCIAL MEDIA JUSTICE..!

There was an incident in Kerala where a pregnant elephant was killed in Malappuram years ago, and a woman in Bangalore was attacked by a Zomato delivery man.
In both cases, social media played a crucial role. Which is...
Media manipulated reality!!!
Thousands of people believed the wrong statements spread in the media. Even politicians, writers, and celebrities tweeted, believing the fake news.
This is called social media justice. Whenever a crisis happens, some junkies try to grab the attention of the mob by manipulating or adding some "masala" to the reality to make it more interesting. And we just express our support and points of view based on these fakes.
There are thousands of other stories where the the media manipulated the real story, and people still believe what the media found in their minds.
I think making an opinion just based on some social media posts or tags is worthless...

CHAPTER EIGHTEEN

THE 0.001% GROUP

There are more than 700 crore people on this planet. But we have only seen a small, tiny part of it. Just a few thousand people. Among them, a few hundred know our identity, and we know a little bit about them too. Maybe a few people know about our family and our true personality. But only a small, tiny part of this large count has spent some meaningful time with us.

Yes, it is true.

We have met so many, but just a few people live in our minds.

When we compare the number of people who live in our minds to the entire planet, it is less than 0.001%, right?

And those people are our people!

The ones who made us laugh, helped, supported, prayed for, and cared about us. This group consists of family, friends, teachers, and many more.

I think each and every individual has that 0.001% group.

Be grateful for their time and presence! Just be grateful for them!

CHAPTER NINETEEN

THEORY OF COMPARISON

The worst thing is to compare ourselves with others. Everyone has their own past, their own point of view about their life, habits, and relationships. Even two kids of the same age growing up in the same family may have distinct virtues. In the same way, each and every one of us has our own privileges and negatives too.

We can find someone with similar backgrounds, experiences, and similarities in many things, but they are not the same as us.

So, is it wise to compare yourself with others?

The only thing that we can compare with is our yesterdays. Are we better than our yesterdays? That matters the most!

The lessons from yesterday, experiences, people, and places-do they make us better or bitter?

CHAPTER TWENTY

THE 3D EXPERIENCE

Experience can be divided into two categories: 2D and 3D. 2D experience comes mainly from the stories of others, books, podcasts, biographies, etc. 3D experience is the experience we gain from our own lives. This includes group activities, taking responsibilities, and engaging in risky tasks.

The 3D experience has a greater impact than the 2D experience because it helps build our personality.

The only way to gain more 3D experience is to engage with society.

Many of us still struggle with social isolation as an effect of the pandemic.

Get more social, make friends, engage in activities, and step out of your house, especially away from your screens. Limit your home to a few purposes like resting and eating. Because the world is always outside...

CHAPTER TWENTY-ONE

THE BEST REWARD IS THE WORK ITESLF

I have been interested in videography since I was 19. I captured some promotional videos for our NSS unit in the beginning using my smartphone. That was cool, and I really enjoyed it.

Then some of my friends approached me to take some event promotion videos. That was a little bit harder: I used a professional camera for the first time and accomplished the task.

Those videos were liked by so many, and that was followed by brand promotions, Reels, and so on.

One day, our guest lecturer approached me and sent me a contact of a director who was in search of an assistant director. Out of curiosity, I made a resume and sent it to him.

Boom. Yeah... then the call came from him!

I joined as an assistant director. I skipped a week of college and roamed all over Palakkad. At that shooting location, I met a bunch of artists and collaborated with them too. I learned filmmaking, screen acting, and many more skills.

After the completion of each work, there were so many appreciations, rewards, and likes.

After each work, I was assigned to a new one, much heavier than the previous one. I think that is the best reward!

It was the best realization that I ever had. The best reward for work is the work itself.

The praise of others and likes on social media were just garbage.

The real reward was the work and the self-satisfaction from doing it!

CHAPTER TWENTY-TWO

THE IDENTITY EFFECT

At a party, there was a man who was just talking with his friends and enjoying himself. Then one of his friends offered him a drink, and he replied, "Dude, I'm trying to quit drinking." The rest of his friends started laughing.
"Really? Okay, just take two sips, bro..."
Then there was another man who replied to his friend, "I don't drink."
The difference is that the first one left the party wearing the crown of "the best drinker of the night," while the second one remained clean until the end.
Here comes the identity effect. When you commit to something like building an aesthetic body, learning music, or quitting alcohol, your identity plays a crucial role.
Try this:
"I'm trying to build my body." Nah!! "I'm an athlete."
"I'm practicing music." Nah!! "I'm a musician."
"I'm trying to quit alcohol." Nah!! "I don't drink."
When you make an identity of the person you want to become, your body will also respond accordingly.

CHAPTER TWENTY-THREE

Cheat Code For No Fap...!!!

99.9% of men fap daily. That's why there is a myth about 90 days of no fap, which is not practical at all. The method is highly based on results, not on the process!

"1 week of no fap, you will become attractive. 1 month, you are an Alpha now... 3 months, you are in the top 1%. And if you relapse, then all the gains will be gone...."

This is not real at all!!!

For someone who faps daily, it's hard to stop in just one day. There is an alternate method for it. Just mark on the calendar how many days you fapped in a month.

If it is more than 25, try to reduce it to 20 next month. Then 15, then 10... And it is hard. Sometimes we get stuck in the 20s or 10s for a long period of time, and that is okay. Someday (maybe years later), there comes a point where you forget about it and you haven't fapped a single time in a month!

The real benefit is not the amount of testosterone that you store in your balls...

It's the confidence, attractiveness, comfort while dealing with women, and a big self-image.

CHAPTER TWENTY-FOUR

Theory Of Introverts

Being social is effortless when you're with the right people.
And mind numbing when you're with the wrong ones.
You're probably not an introvert, your friends just suck.
Even the most introverted person will want to stay late at dinner when the conversation is great.
"An American introvert is an English extrovert." George Mack
So if you would be more extroverted if you'd been born in America, or in a more social family, or had a more outgoing friend group, what does it mean to say you are an introvert?
Stack on top of that if you're not particularly fired up or interested by the people around you, or if you're currently going through a Lonely Chapter where you're outgrowing your old friends of course you're not going to feel particularly extroverted.
Don't be gaslit by cultural conditioning and misaligned friends masquerading as intrinsic nature.
You're probably not an introvert, your friends just suck.

THOUGHTS OF A TEENAGER

Credits: 3MM

CHAPTER TWENTY-FIVE

THE SIGMA MALE

Sigma males don't date. Sigma males have a terrible attitude.

Sigmas are introverts.

A meme of Christian Bale from American Psycho ruled in the media.

What is the reality of it? Do they really exist?

Theoretically, there is a social hierarchy consisting of Alpha, Beta, and so on, in which Sigma stays out of it all.

They are supposed to be lone wolves.

But the truth is, when winter comes, the lone wolf dies alone. The pack survives.

Having a toxic mentality against the opposite sex, lifelong introversion, and not caring about your surroundings doesn't make you powerful and extraordinary but a pathetic psycho.

In order to get some views and likes, some junkies spread this trend, and many adopted it too (which is ridiculous right now).

Becoming a man is awesome, but being a Sigma is just...

CHAPTER TWENTY-SIX

BEING INFJ

As an INFJ, I always struggled to make new friends.
I thought my ideology of friendship was cringe.
I made most of my friends from the group that I worked with. When I work with someone, I can measure their work ethic, commitment, honesty, humility, helpfulness, discipline, and many other qualities.
As a result, my friend circle was too small. Sometimes it took years to form a genuine bond with a friend. I thought it was boring.
But there was a pretty side to it too...
The roots of each and every friendship were too deep. These were long-lasting friendships. They were present at my highs as well as lows. When I look at my close circle, which consists of an entrepreneur, athlete, photographer, violinist...
Once I hated this trait!
But then I realized it is the quality that matters, not the quantity!
Having a few people with a full heart is much better than a mob with less commitment, right?

CHAPTER TWENTY-SEVEN

3 Types Of Men

According to the Geeta, three types of men exist: Swathika, Rajasa, and Thamasa. They behave differently in their work, daily lives, and relationships.

Swathika men never expect any kind of reward for their work, a concept referred to as "Thyaga." Rajasa men take rewards for their work; in fact, they work for the outcome. Thamasa men devote their work to humiliating others, which includes betrayal, dishonesty, and many other negative behaviors.

These three types also have different diets. The first type, Swathika, eats food rich in fruits, vegetables, and healthy fats. men eat both vegetarian and non-vegetarian foods that are spicy or baked, sometimes consuming food that has been kept for days. Thamasa men have a habit of eating dead and unclean food, alcohol, and contaminated foods.

The life of a Swastika is always considered to be an ideal life, free from cravings and modern-world degeneracy. It is challenging to live like a Swastika in modern times.

However, they are the ones who experience the power of "Parabrahma" and eventually attain "Moksha."

CHAPTER TWENTY-EIGHT

TRUTH ABOUT EXAMS

In India, there are numerous competitive exams such as IIT JEE, NEET, GATE, and UPSC, among others. Parents are often brainwashed into believing that these exams are the only path to a successful career. As a result, they blindly send their children to coaching centers, investing lakhs of rupees and 2-3 years of their children's lives to crack these exams.

However, this belief is not always accurate.

After completing my +2, I was also one of those students who spent thousands on coaching centers with the aim of securing a seat at IIT Madras for Aerospace Engineering. I joined a famous coaching center and committed myself to cracking the exam, studying 8-10 hours a day, with no interaction with the external world and no rest or relaxation. Despite my efforts, I couldn't succeed in my first attempt. I planned to dedicate one more year to preparation, but my parents refused.

In hindsight, that was a wise decision, and I am truly grateful for it. During that year, my mental health had deteriorated significantly.

If you are planning to prepare for any competitive exams and invest years of time and lakhs of rupees in the hope of building a career, consider alternative options.

Try dropshipping, email marketing, real estate, or video editing, which offer career opportunities outside of the conventional matrix.

Otherwise, you may end up as another participant in a competition of the blind, fitting into a corrupted system.

CHAPTER TWENTY-NINE

JUST DIVE IN

There were two groups of photographers. The first group aimed to take at least 30 photos each day, while the second group focused on capturing just one perfect photo each day. After a period of time, they analyzed the quality of their photos. Surprisingly, the photos from the first group were far better than those from the second group.

This demonstrates that in order to master something, you must engage in it regularly without obsessing over perfection. Consistent practice leads to improvement and eventually perfection.

For instance, if you want to learn swimming, it's more effective to spend 30 minutes in the pool daily rather than watching instructional videos for 29 days and attempting to swim on the 30th day.

The only way to truly master a skill is by doing it, not merely by planning, forecasting, or learning the theories. Just dive in and do it.

CHAPTER THIRTY

Modern Wisdom

Which of my current values would be different if I were raised by different parents?
What do I think is ambition (a good trait) but is actually envy (a terrible one)?
What annoys me about other people that I sometimes do myself?
How much of my nostalgia is a false or incomplete memory of the past?
Is there something in my life I think I'm "passionate" about or "focused" on but I'm actually just addicted to it?
Do I spend more time defending what I already know instead of trying to learn something new?
Are there people in my life who I consider kind and compassionate but they're actually just too shy to tell me hard truths?
What would Instagram look like if it were an honest reflection of people's life, instead of a curated highlight reel?
Am I being as nice as I could be, rather than just as nice as I need to be.

THOUGHTS OF A TEENAGER

Credits: 3MM

CHAPTER THIRTY-ONE

The Modern Problem

After a long time, I went with my brother to see a movie during his vacation. The movie was titled "Premalu." The performances were good, engaging, and funny. When I left the theater, I felt some of it was too real...

Completing Engineering and having no idea what to do next Preparing for IIT to reunite with a girlfriend Having no idea about GATE, but still going to coaching Working hard to get a pretty girl with no purpose or concern about one's own life Finally going abroad in the hope of a better future...

The film was a good entertainer, but the director also had a keen vision of modern men.

CHAPTER THIRTY-TWO

THE PRIVATE SPACE

During the final year of our graduation, we were allotted single rooms in our hostel. After three months, I noticed that a person's character was often reflected in the state of their room.

The room opposite mine belonged to Rishikesh, who was well-disciplined and humble. As with his character, his room was clean and neat. The books were well-organized on the shelf, and he had a to-do list on his wall.

Another person, Agri, was an entrepreneur in charge of several communities. His room was full of sticky notes on the wall, Arduino boards, and various equipment, but everything was in its place.

However, some rooms had a dirty, disgusting smell and were full of cigarettes and bottles.

Even if a person seems nice and good, just check their private space and how they manage it; that reveals their real character, not the one they show to the external world.

CHAPTER THIRTY-THREE

CREDIT TAKERS

There are some men
Who Always says...
I did this I made this I'm the one who
But in reality the one who does all this never takes the credit for it. They just do and leave, they are not supposed to get appreciation by doing it.
Remember if someone mentions any of the above, they are the cowards!!!!
I learned this lesson during the cultural fest of our college during 2022 from a senior that I respected the most.
He popularized himself as the best one. But in reality he was a dump just sitting out there, doing nothing. But he was there for every group photo, every publicity event, every poster and medias but during work he was just sitting in the chair.
They make the image for themselves and seek external validation.
Kind of mental mastrubation...!
some of the mob get manipulated by it(for a short time), not everyone!!!
In reality they are losing respect..!.

CHAPTER THIRTY-FOUR

BEING A NICE GUY

There is a group of men referred to as "nice guys."
They behave the way society expects them to.
For a nice guy, he:
Helps too much
Cares too much
Loves too much
If this particular group of men encounters any toxic surroundings, they are going to suffer.
They will squeeze his blood and tear him apart.
That's for sure...
Being humble, honest, loving, and caring are good virtues, but the label of "too much" can destroy you.
Always maintain a limit because not everyone deserves it.
Otherwise, this "too much" can hurt you so much.

CHAPTER THIRTY-FIVE

How To Remove Bad Habits

We often end up with bad things because of the pleasure that we get from it. In Fact the dopamine spikes... but later it makes pain. Pain of low self esteem, bad self image too. Imagine you are consuming alcohol or porn, in the very beginning you feel much enjoyment but later on, your body and mind behave like dump, you realize the fact that you are not doing good, do you feel grateful after watching a full lengthy xxx video and jerking off for 5 times??
Nahh...
You spoil your self image, your mental health and productivity too.
We are much addicted to the initial pleasure only..
But how to stop it???
We are doing it again because our body is having little good quality dopamine.
Good dopamine??
It comes from the reverse of the earlier... Just opposite: pain in the beginning and pleasure in the later.. Which include the following habits: Meditation, journaling, exercises, cold showers.

All these are hard to do, that is the beauty of it... The pain is much heavier in the beginning..that's why we skip it!
But the pleasure comes just wait, do it for a few days you can
feel the presence of good quality dopamine...
Which eventually eliminates the bad dopamine cravings too......
So Never focus on eliminating those bad habits, just make some good habits.

CHAPTER THIRTY-SIX

THE NEET SCAM

Well the total score of 720, if you hit the right option you got the 4 marks, if it's wrong it is -1 then and if you didn't attempt it then it is 0. But during this year's NEET exam many candidates got 719,718,717 marks too.

It is practically not possible, but happens in INDIA.
Because if you pay the right people with the right things you can score well, you can get jobs and even promotions too.

The one who worked hard, committed their time and took effort just stays on the bench.

Because education is a business nowadays, the coaching centers, exam boards are making enough monetary benefits.

But many students lose their mental health, money and hope.

And the reality is, we are still encouraging the rise of suicidal spots like Kota!!

CHAPTER THIRTY-SEVEN

50% GOD THOEREM

In every exam season there is an outdated comedy of 50% God and his power..
"Thaan paathi daivam paathi"
Does that really happen? Because I Never felt it.
I have never passed any exam without studying, never won a karate fight without practice, never earned respect without hard work!
Because it is always 99% you and 1% God! He helps the one who works hard, studies hard...
He is not going to solve the problems for you until you try yourself to overcome them.
I still remember the day when our Glorie teacher taught the lesson from a Hindi doha which is
"hey priest open your eyes, the one you're praying for is not in the stone, he is with the men who work hard on the field"

CHAPTER THIRTY-EIGHT

THE SOCIAL MEDIA...!

Imagine you have got a job in Abu Dhabi. And you decided to go to a luxurious pub with your friends. As you get there you saw a young billionaire entering to the pub with some pretty girls, he had a Rolex on his hand with a roaring Lambo..
(like Bruce Wayne)
And after a few minutes you realized that most people out there were millionaires.
how do you feel then?
You become jealous and your mind will be at the peak of Envy.
Social media does the same too..
Everybody's having fun, going to parties, trips, chilling out and you sitting out there scrolling and watching it like a little monkey.
not satisfied with your life, ruined health and mind and living like a dumb.
And the funniest part is most of them go to the nature to capture pictures rather healing, go to the gym to show of rather than building muscles.

Because in this digital revolution, there is no other tool than media to Brian wash us!!!

CHAPTER THIRTY-NINE

READ MORE...

It was October 2022 and I was spending my final year at college. Spending time with friends just hanging out and Eager to do something productive well, sounds cliche right??
and i realized, behind every successful personality they have a thing in common which is reading !!!!
From ImanGadzhi to King Khan they had a good collection of books ,some of them read a book per week !!
inspired from all these giants started from Robinsharma. well in my case it was from just a single paragraph in each night then a page then a chapter so on..
now i got a few more companions Ryan Holiday,Marcus Arelius,James clear .. and let me ask you one question
Do you have the courage to read a paragraph in a day??
if you had it then......
welcome to the 1% club.

CHAPTER FORTY

FEEL YOUR FEELINGS

Feeling stuck is feeling stuck.
Feeling pain is feeling pain.
Feeling abandonment is feeling abandonment.

Only the one who is in that state knows the intensity of it not an outsider, even if it's a friend, a loved one, or your own mother.

The thing is, it hurts more for the person going through it than for the audience watching....

CHAPTER FORTY-ONE

CAREER...!

Focus on the career nothing else.. is the worst advice you can give to a youngster..

Only studies, exams and jobs are never going to give you a life of joy and happiness. Because it is a mixture of many more..

We are often brainwashed in such a way that getting a good job or High status career has become the ultimate criteria for fulfillment.

Even if you have achieved everything and you are alone?

If you lose your mental health and physical fitness for it.

Lost your family and relations too??

Does that make any sense??

In search of fulfillment the many of us lost ourselves. We became alone, unsatisfied and looked for some sort of pills to get fulfillment.

Remember we need a healthy body, Peaceful mind, good relationships and a purpose for our well being. If you're losing any of it for a so-called career, you are losing a part of yourself too.!

CHAPTER FORTY-TWO

POWER OF NOW!!

I will start studying after the match. I will do the assignment after lunch. I will implement the plan after this Sunday.

Waiting for the perfect moment is fine, but many times we expect the perfect time in future then it never happens. Plan the studies to begin 1 month before the exams and start at the morning of examination day.

Plan to start a habit on the sunday but which Sunday? You never mentioned it.

I will start the business after 40? But will you live till your 40? Do you have a guarantee for it?

If you are free, and able to do it. Then the only solution is to do it.

That's why Tink believes in the principle of now or never!!!

CHAPTER FORTY-THREE

LET'S TALK ABOUT WOMEN!!

Women are simple but...
Let's talk with some examples, A women prefers friendship, togetherness and love over everything
But for a man it is the status and power that matters!!
Women love praising!! On their looks, dressing... They like external validation! But they like it only if it is genuine!
Sometimes they don't mean what they say.
Imagine you are a soldier and you are leaving behind your wife to rejoining the battalion.
She will cry for you: don't go, please..
And if you respond like: okey babe, I'm not going, let my friends take care of the borders..
Do you think she will keep the same respect after that??
Never...
Imagine you made millions but you just forgot to pay the cable bill. She will definitely be mad at you. And you: "Babe, now I can buy an entire satellite but you are concerned about the cable.." But that is not going to convince her. It is the cable bill that you didn't pay..

And the last thing is none of my lady viewers are not going to accept the above mentioned traits.
Because they are... Women!!

CHAPTER FORTY-FOUR

Choosing The Right Pain

Choosing a job based solely on salary or benefits is shortsighted because every job comes with its own privileges and pains.

Consider the life of an Army officer: the attractive salary, the royal villa, the executive car, and the respect from society. You might see some mass media motivational or inspirational shorts and reels featuring a well-uniformed officer walking with an M416 in his hand, accompanied by dramatic background music.

But the reality is that he is protecting the borders at Siachen in -14 degrees, facing bullets and grenades in militant areas, and sacrificing his own family and life for the country. He doesn't care about the cool car or luxury villa. It is that pain and discomfort that made him a soldier.

Every discipline has its own problems and struggles. Raising a business is hard and frustrating. Teaching students is physically and mentally exhausting. Acting in front of a camera for hours, maintaining emotions until the director calls cut, is hard. Everything has its own pain. But if you are unable to choose the right pain that suits you,

you will end up shifting jobs and careers.
Choose the right pain-the one you can bear and feel awful while enduring it.

CHAPTER FORTY-FIVE

BRAINWASHED CULT

Yesterday, I saw some of my friends talking about the celebrities who made huge donations for the Wayanad tragedy. Some of them were praising it because their idol made the biggest donation! Then they talked about the cars these celebrities had, their apartments, and so on.

We are much more concerned about them. We are more concerned about their relationships than ours, their kids than ours, and their houses than ours. This is because we are brainwashed by the media.

There is a famous quote from the movie Fight Club: "Murder, crime, poverty-these things don't concern me. What concerns me are celebrity magazines, television with 500 channels, some guy's name on my underwear. Rogaine, Viagra, Olestra..."

Yeah, it is true. We are brainwashed by the media, politicians, and society.

Remember, if your parents are still going for a 9-5 job and struggling to pay the bills, there is no point in focusing on others and their lives. Just save yourself first!

CHAPTER FORTY-SIX

LIFE OF AN EAGLE

"Every eagle, at around 40 years old, faces a life- altering decision. Its once powerful beak and talons have grown weak and brittle, and its majestic feathers no longer support its flight. The eagle must make a choice: endure a painful process of renewal or succumb to a slow, inevitable decline.

The eagle retreats to a high mountain top and begins the arduous process of self-renewal. It plucks out its old, weakened feathers, one by one. The pain is intense, but the eagle knows that without shedding the old, there can be no new growth.

Next, the eagle breaks off its beak by striking it against a rock. This excruciating step is necessary for a new, stronger beak to grow. The pain is profound, yet it is a pain of purpose, a pain that heralds a new beginning.

Finally, the eagle claws out its old talons, making way for new ones to take their place. With each painful step, the eagle moves closer to rebirth, closer to reclaiming its strength and majesty.

After months of struggle and suffering, the eagle emerges renewed, ready to soar once again. This powerful transformation is a testament to the strength and resilience within us all. Pain is not just a byproduct of change; it is the very catalyst that drives us to grow, to evolve, and to reach new heights."

CHAPTER FORTY-SEVEN

THE BATMAN

Why Tink likes Batman over any other comic character: The reason is he is a superhero without any superpowers.

The trauma of losing his parents in his childhood, 8 years of solitude, and the search for the meaning of his life, a mentality of true justice which transformed the young billionaire into Batman.

And the villain Joker also had the trauma of losing his pregnant wife. He considered it a bad joke and chose to give everyone else the same pain, ending up like a psychopath.

But Batman,

He never kills anyone. He is strict with his discipline and committed to a purpose. He is wealthy, both in terms of money and technology. Yet, the billionaire orphan had only one concern: his city Gotham.

Because he believed:

"Our scars can destroy us, even after the physical wounds have healed. But if we survive them, they can transform us. They can give us the power to endure and the strength to fight."

Both the heroes and villains experience some sort of pain, but it is their choice: to help someone who faces the same pain or spread the same pain they felt.

CHAPTER FORTY-EIGHT

How To Read A Book

We all read books. But how do we read them properly?
The first time you read a new book, it is entirely fresh content for your brain, and the brain won't be able to catch the whole concept.
Read it again. Now you can get the true meaning of it.
Now?
Read it once again. Now you are not reading; you are learning it. You can write a short book from the book, take a lecture on the book, or deliver a course on the book.
And if you can write a sentence from each chapter after the third reading, then you are a pro!
And if you are highly interested in the lessons, then keep the book on your shelf and read it once a year.
Well, anybody can read a book once and skip it, but only a few people learn from it.

CHAPTER FORTY-NINE

THE SPOTLIGHT EFFECT

I knew the name of my grandfather, but I never saw him (he died before my birth). He was tall and tried many businesses too. That's all I knew about him.

Well, after three generations, everyone would be remembered the same way. Perhaps nobody is going to remember your name at all. So is there any point in taking action based on external judgment? Even your own family is not going to remember you after three generations, and neither will society.

We often misunderstand that everybody is watching us, focusing on us as if we are in the middle of a spotlight. But everyone is busy with their own business.

If you get an Olympic medal, for them it is just: congrats.

And what if you lose your limb? It is just: ooh.

Then they move on to their own worlds and their own priorities.

So taking any decision based on external judgment has no importance at all. Ninety percent of people feel the spotlight effect. As a result, we end up with a life we hate:

THOUGHTS OF A TEENAGER

the job which has high social status but less personal satisfaction, the dress which is stylish but uncomfortable to wear, the bike which has a fierce look but you can't take your mom on the back seat, and so on.

You are not in the spotlight because it never exists at all..

CHAPTER FIFTY

Diet

It is not about eating less but eating clean.
There are mainly three hormones related to our appetite: insulin, ghrelin, and leptin.
Insulin helps in the absorption of glucose and can also influence fat storage. Leptin is the hormone that signals to reduce hunger, and ghrelin is the hormone that signals hunger.
The problem with junk food is that it induces more insulin, which can interfere with leptin signaling, making us eat more even when the stomach is full. If you eat a meal at 1 PM every day, ghrelin will be produced at the same time, making you feel hungry at that time.
All foods contain calories, but the effect of food on hormone production matters more. That is the point of eating clean. By avoiding processed foods, you can maintain a healthy balance of these hormones, leading to healthier eating habits...

CHAPTER FIFTY-ONE

MONK MODE

Monk mode is a temporary form of MGTOW, by cutting yourself off from the rest of the world for a while you can fine-tune your focus, calibrate your direction and confront yourself.

You'll be acknowledging your weaknesses and then formulating a plan of action to deal with them." The focus is on "minimizing your time contribution to social obligations and junk activities because these consume much of your time whilst yielding little to negligible increase towards your social market value. Monk mode is a serious commitment that is not to be half-assed.

You're either doing it, or you're not

The problem is that Monk Mode justifies a retreat from life, risk taking and adventure as self development.

It makes you feel noble in isolation.

So much so that it can become hard to bring yourself back out.

This means that if you already have a tendency to live a sheltered, unsocial life, you're encouraging yourself to abscond even further away from ever building a real-life support network - the thing which you actually need most in the long run.

So Periodise.!!!!
Set a deadline for your Monk Mode to end. 3-6 months is a sweet spot in my experience. Do longer if you've not done it before, shorter if you're further along your journey.
Credits: Iman & Chris

CHAPTER FIFTY-TWO

THE GEN Z

What is Gen Z? Let me explain...
Generation X (Gen X) Birth Years: Roughly 1965 to 1980
Generation Y (Gen Y), also known as Millennials Birth Years: Roughly 1981 to 1996
Generation Z (Gen Z) Birth Years: Roughly 1997 to 2012

Gen Z are the ones who have grown up with technology. They are faster, follow trends, and know about global issues more than any other generation.

But the problem with Gen Z is they have poor mental health. Despite being digitally connected, many in Gen Z report feelings of loneliness and social isolation, lacking deep and meaningful real-world connections. The suicide rates and addictions are higher among them too. Poor mental health is not always depression or anxiety.

If you are addicted to anything, like any type of food, media, or bad habits such as oversleeping or excessive screen time, and you can't control it, then you also have a poor mind. And Gen Z has all of it.

Remember, these are not the reasons for poor mental health; they are the symptoms! Like a downward spiral, poor mental health leads to bad habits, and bad habits lead to poor mental health.

And how to rectify it?

The best step is to reduce screen time. For me, it was 5 hours a day, and now I'm able to manage it for 3 hours and try my best to control it for 1 hour.

1. Use extensions like Unhook for removing shorts from YouTube.
2. Set a time limit for Instagram.
3. Customize the notification bar.
4. Clean the app store.

Like a gooseberry, it is sour in the beginning and sweet in the end.

CHAPTER FIFTY-THREE

THE GAGAN BOYS

During 2020, was working in a startup named Gagan Aerospace. Under a few hardworking seniors-Gokul , Alok , and Anuranj -they were so incredible in their work that I wasn't able to finish the deadlines many times with them.

From morning to noon, I had online classes, and then after, I worked with Gagan. The entire COVID era was just productive. Those legends were working 12-14 hours a day!

After COVID, when college reopened, I met the lead, Gokul , for the very first time at MH. I said, "Hey Gokul , I'm Ajay, I was..." Gokul Ettan replied, "Eda, actually I haven't washed this uniform for 3 weeks, so can we meet after some time?"

In between work, he forgot to wash his uniform for weeks.. Saved his name as Gokul Elon Musk in my phone. He was like an alien.

But they were never recognized for the work they put in, because they didn't expect it.

And there was another incident....

During the time of the film fest, the worst comment I heard was from my best boy. He was assigned to a responsible position and had many tasks. His mentality was different: "I have no duties, right? Just show up and sit there...ha!!Well, if you want to just sit in a position, go to a nearby park and sit there. Don't use the chair of a manager or president for it.

Well, for some men like the Gagan boys, the position doesn't matter. They don't want any reward or recognition. They grind even if they are not recognized for it. They push even if they fail. They work even if it has no results. Because they are the type of men mentioned in the Geetha as "the Sthithapranja."

CHAPTER FIFTY-FOUR

LISTENERS

Anybody can talk, but not everybody can be a good listener.

When I was at my lowest during 2022, my right shoulder joint dislocated twice, I got hit by food poisoning and found it difficult even to drink water, and I lost body weight. After the recovery, I had an injury on my right leg ligament and struggled to walk. My body was so damaged. I still remember those days when I struggled to appear for the semester exams and performed so poorly in the labs.

Well, it wasn't the end. The real problem started after a week. The failed relationship, problems with my friends and co-workers, political issues in the clubs and communities, betrayal from a beloved friend- all these eventually tore me apart! I was mentally ruined. I was so pathetic in the positions that I was assigned, so weak in the project group. Seeing my poor performance, the teachers removed me from the positions, the project group members were angry at me, and my academics suffered.

The CGPA of 9.24 went down to 8.17, affecting my placements, extracurricular activities, and I struggled to follow my daily tasks too. The back-to-back tragedies made me alone and eventually brought me into trauma.

I decided to take a course break. As an engineering student, there is an option for applying for a course break and using that time to work on a startup. But it was my group tutor who supported me to continue my studies. During all this time, I tried to talk with my friends and explain my problems, but some of them helped me, but they had their own priorities. They listened for a while and then went back to their own worlds. For them, I was just "Ooh, here comes the sad boy."

But during all these tragedies, the one who listened to me was my mum! Because in her world, I was the first priority!!! The best therapist that I had spent my time with.

For everybody else, you are an outsider. There is only limited time for you. But for your parents, the priority is you! If somebody says, "You can't explain every problem to your parents," my answer is, "Yes, it is possible! In fact, your relationship with your family is poor, brother." Your friends may not donate an organ for you, but your parents can. Because they are the ones who can listen to you for hours, as they are the ones who listened to you from your first cry!

CHAPTER FIFTY-FIVE

LEARN A NEW SKILL

So, you're starting something new and learning new skills, huh? It's a great idea to take advice from someone who's already nailed it. But here's the kicker: don't just copy their current game plan. Think about it. You're at level 0, trying to get to level 10, while they're at level 80, aiming for level 100. It's a whole different ball game!

At level 0, you're swimming in a sea of fear, self-doubt, and anxiety. Meanwhile, those pros have a treasure chest full of knowledge and experience. Starting out is tough because you're wrestling with your own insecurities and learning to walk before you run.

But guess what? This is your time to make all the hilarious, cringe-worthy mistakes you want. It's your freedom to fail, learn, and laugh at yourself. Embrace the chaos of the beginning.

CHAPTER FIFTY-SIX

HOW татTo Learn A Language

When I was a kid, our TV had only 60 channels, and 57 of them were in Hindi. Naturally, I ended up watching a lot of Hindi movies and TV shows. By the age of 10, I was speaking Hindi so fluently. All credit goes to the Star Utsav channel and its legendary programs like Sonpari, Shakalaka Boom Boom, and the Sunday movies.

But then there was English... Oh, English. I tried reading newspapers, but that didn't work out so well. I'd just look at the pictures on the sports page and call it a day. Fast forward to 2019, and I started watching Hollywood horror movies-The Conjuring, Annabelle, Insidious, Recc and let's just say my vocabulary expanded in the most terrifying way possible. During COVID, my phone was ruled by web series like Game of Thrones, Peaky Blinders, Vikings, and Lost. My vocabulary, word power, and fluency went through a total transformation. I mean, how could they not? With Thomas Shelby, Ivar the Boneless, and Desmond Hume as my unofficial English tutors, I was bound to pick up a few things!

After that, I started listening to podcasts, which took my word game to the next level. My pronunciation improved too-no more saying "pronounciation" instead of "pronunciation" (who knew, right?).

Now, I can deliver a speech in English like a pro, and write an essay? Pfft, that's child's play. When I attend interviews, I don't even think twice about my language skills-I've already leveled up!

In my humble opinion, the best way to learn a language is by consuming content. Movies, songs, series-they really do the trick! Then, sure, go ahead and hit the books, grammar too. But starting with a journal or newspaper? Not the best move. Start with something that entertains you, something that keeps you hooked.

Because at the end of the day, we learn it because we enjoy it!

CHAPTER FIFTY-SEVEN

MODERATE SPEED

Imagine you are traveling to Palakkad from Thrissur on a bike. If you speed up to 70 km h for the entire journey, the piston of your bike is going to burn out..! And if you go at 30 kmph, you won't reach your destination on time. Going too slow or too fast can be destructive. We need a moderate speed of 45 kmph with enough breaks.

Try this with everything, especially in the gym, studies, and daily routine.

Remember, this is only applicable to longer-term activities. We have to adjust according to the urgency too.

Because everything is not a marathon always And the story of the rabbit and tortoise is not always applicable. If it were a fox instead of a rabbit, the story would have a different climax.

CHAPTER FIFTY-EIGHT

LEARN TO LIMIT

"How to Win Friends and Influence People" is a book by Dale Carnegie that has built a massive fanbase for its advice on building relationships. You can find a ton of guidance on making good relationships, friendships, and mentorships. However, it's equally important to limit some of your connections in a healthy way.

Because, as Rocky said, "The world is not all sunshine and rainbows..."

If you're an empath, you might find yourself trapped in a circle of toxic people. While we can't change them, we can limit our exposure to them. How? By mastering the art of saying no.

If you feel that any of your friends, relatives, or colleagues are not good for you, cut them off, ignore them. Don't sacrifice yourself to fit in. There are plenty of good people out there who will accept you as you are and who will smile because of your presence.

If you're struggling with any of your connections, then it's not a connection at all-it's a Destruction

CHAPTER FIFTY-NINE

DECISIONS

Struggling to make decisions?
Well
Option 1: follow your heart. Here comes the decisions based on your emotions and feelings.
Option 2: follow your brain, which is full of logic and practicality.
Which will you choose??

CHAPTER SIXTY

Understanding Sleep: The Difference Between Bedtime and Sleep Time

It's a common misconception that the amount of time you spend in bed equals the amount of sleep you get. However, this isn't the case. For instance, if you go to bed at 10 PM and wake up at 5 AM, you might assume you've had 7 hours of sleep. But in reality, your body doesn't fall asleep instantly when you lie down. It typically takes some time to transition from wakefulness to sleep, and during the night, you may wake up briefly without even realizing it.

These factors mean that the actual time you're asleep (sleep time) is often less than the total time you spend in bed (bed time).

Your body goes through a series of physiological changes to prepare for sleep, one of which is a drop in body temperature. This cooling down process is essential for reaching deeper stages of sleep, where the body and mind undergo the most restorative processes. This is why we often find it harder to wake up on cold mornings, particularly during the winter or rainy seasons-our body temperature is already low, making us want to stay asleep.

A cooler sleeping environment can actually help you fall asleep faster and enjoy deeper sleep. This is because your body's core temperature naturally decreases when you sleep, and a cool room can aid in this process. However, the optimal room temperature for sleep varies from person to person, but it's generally recommended to keep your bedroom cool, around 60-67°F (15-19°C).

If you're aiming for 7 hours of actual sleep, it's wise to plan for 8 hours of bed time. This extra hour accounts for the time it takes to fall asleep initially, any brief awakenings during the night, and the time it takes to fully wake up in the morning. For example, if you need to wake up at 6 AM, it's a good idea to be in bed by 10 PM. This ensures that you give your body enough time to cycle through the necessary stages of sleep to feel refreshed and well-rested.

CHAPTER SIXTY-ONE

LESSONS FROM DEAR ZINDAGI

Be honest with yourself: It's okay to make mistakes, but don't be too hard on yourself and criticize yourself too much.

Express yourself: It's okay to put on a strong face sometimes, but it's better to express yourself.

Seek mental health: The movie emphasizes the importance of mental health and that the brain is part of the body that may need help too. It also tries to change the mindset that only crazy people seek mental help and that it's okay to consult someone even for everyday issues.

Don't let your past ruin your future: Your unresolved past can haunt your present and hinder you from fully embracing life and forming meaningful relationships.

Be open to love: Love your life and see how happy you can be.

Take the steering wheel of your life: You are your own teacher in the school of life.

Celebrate imperfection: The movie celebrates the beauty of imperfection and the journey of self- discovery.

CHAPTER SIXTY-TWO

THE CIRCUMSTANCES

Well, it was the final year of my graduation, and I was in charge of the film fest. Due to many political problems, I was constantly in dispute with our tech fest coordinator, Devsuraj, my classmate, and my hostel mate, Devan!
And our common friends struggled in between us. We were like a dog and a cat, hard to live under the same roof.
After graduation, when I shifted to Chennai, Ramapuram, it was the same Devan with whom I spent almost 7 months in an apartment.
Both of us were working as Application Engineers, leading professional careers! None of our friends and family members believed that I was with him.
And when I told him about this, he responded with the same answer-that none of his mates did either...
We roamed around Chennai, discussed those tragedies, went to the beach, cooked together, and I have never spent such wonderful days with any of my mates.
Well, at one point, the one with whom I struggled the most became my brother!!

Why did it happen?
Because of the circumstances... It was the circumstances that made a bitter relationship, not the people. He was the most genuine and polite guy I ever met. And the best lesson was that at some point, some may break us and tear us apart, but not everyone who argues with you is your enemy, and the one who shakes hands with you is not necessarily your friend!!
Rather than blaming people, we can simply blame the circumstances, right?

CHAPTER SIXTY-THREE

ANYBODY CAN FAKE THEIR OWN CHARACTER

They can post a photo in the gym and pretend to be an athlete...

Take a photo with a pet and seem to be a good caretaker... Talk about some quotes on Instagram and act like a philosopher...

If you want to check the real character of a person, just look into their private things-especially their room and their close friends.

I have never seen an undisciplined man with a tidy room. I have never seen a CEO with bad friends.

Your table, the items in your fridge, and your closet are reflections of your inner self. And your close connections are the people you aspire to be.

You can also try it in reverse-if you want to become an entrepreneur, surround yourself with four entrepreneurs, and you will become the fifth one.

If you want to become disciplined, start by cleaning the mess in your room first...
Like an upward spiral...
The quality inside you reflects in your private space, and the quality of your private space reflects your inner qualities.

CHAPTER SIXTY-FOUR

WARNING...!

Recently, I heard the story of Chris Williamson, who was brutally bullied in school and suffered trauma in his childhood. He became a famous model and club promoter, is running a podcast named "Modern Wisdom," and became an influencer! He became a man of success in his fitness, life, and business too. But even years later, he was still going to therapy for proper healing. Recently, one of his old schoolmates met him and said, "I'm really sorry for that... I was just having fun." And Chris replied,
"It's okay... but it nearly took mylife."
Even years later, his schoolmates knew it was a wrong act. But Chris spent his entire childhood alone, playing with a tennis ball in his room, without socializing, the only child of his parents... However, he survived! But a little part of him still suffers...
When we engage with our friends, we may do some nasty things and put the label of "having fun."
We were young, we were enjoying ourselves...
But what is the point of having fun if it ruins someone's:
1. Mental health
2. Money

3. Trust
4. Emotions
and life...

Is the justification of "having fun" enough?
Remember: for a rapist, it may be a momentary urge, but for the victim, it is an everlasting trauma!
The things that are labeled as "fun" for you may not be the same for everyone.
If somebody is suffering due to the so-called "fun," well, it isn't fun anymore!So, just consider the long-term effects of your actions. Do they lead to better outcomes or bitter

CHAPTER SIXTY-FIVE

The most valuable thing isn't time; it is attention

During the Industrial Revolution, those who invested in firms like steel, oil, and coal made billions, and the situation has changed now. We are living in the digital revolution, where the internet plays a crucial role. In this new era, individual attention has become a source of income. Just look at the internet: when we visit a website, we are bombarded with dozens of ads. Watch a YouTube video, and you'll see recommendations. Google something, and it will follow you around every corner of your online world.

Whether it's about a car, food, or clothing, the ads won't leave you until you engage with their content! Now, Reels and Shorts are designed in such a way that you only need 0.5 seconds to see new content on your screen, often edited with highly curated visuals, music, and captions, making you spend hours on it without even realizing it.

So how can you protect yourself from these modern attention thieves? The best methods are using browser extensions and regularly clearing your browsing history. Extensions can limit recommendations, and clearing your history periodically helps prevent unwanted content from following you around.

While we are all consumers, don't let a manipulative creator take advantage of your valuable time!

CHAPTER SIXTY-SIX

Harder Things....

Just because something is harder to obtain doesn't mean it is valuable.
It's hard to get a Lambo in the driveway...
Hard to make a billion...
Hard to have a supermodel-like girlfriend...
These are hard and attractive, but do we really need them?
What we may actually need are healthy friendships and relationships, mindfulness, purpose, family, and health.
These may seem easier to get in the beginning, but they are harder to maintain in the long run.

CHAPTER SIXTY-SEVEN

THE SPIDER-MAN

Why Are Boys Afraid of Spiders? Since my childhood, the only thing I feared was not my father but the spider that seemed to stare at me from every corner. I don't know why, but whenever I see them, I just run away and try to find a place free from spiders. Even in my early 20s, whenever I see one, my heart rate rises. Why does this happen?

Once, I discussed this with my friends and cousins, and many of them felt the same way but most of them were boys, and they often felt ashamed to admit it! I was a little confused and tried to find an answer. I did some research and found this:

"The fear of spiders is called arachnophobia. Arachnophobia is an intense, irrational fear of spiders and other arachnids (like scorpions). People with arachnophobia often feel anxious or panicked at the sight of a spider or even just thinking about one. This fear can range from mild discomfort to severe terror, leading to avoidance behaviors like refusing to enter rooms where spiders might be present or avoiding activities where spiders might be encountered."

Sometimes, my family and friends have taken advantage of this phobia (toxic behavior, indeed!). From my experience, arachnophobia has no age limit. There are many therapies and treatments available for it too!

Well, whether you have arachnophobia or not, don't play with spiders because not everyone can become Spider-Man, no matter how much we wish we could!

CHAPTER SIXTY-EIGHT

DON'T BURN YOUR ENGINE...!

Hard work pays off, but in the long run, you have to be careful. During my entrance preparation, I was attending classes for hours, then spending more hours studying, with no social interaction, no fun activities, and only 4-5 hours of sleep-just study, study, and study...!

A bunch of books, PYQs, mock tests, and I was... In the midst of this brainwashed exam preparation, I was losing myself!

And what happened? After 6 months, I became drained, hated the whole process, and started giving up. I tried to push even harder, but it eventually made things worse.

Let's look into reality.

We are not robots; we are humans. We need healthy sleep because sleep is the foundation of physical health, mental health, and productivity. If you lose sleep, you won't be able to perform well!

Good relationships are essential for our survival, perhaps the ones that drive us to take on challenging tasks. Maybe a talk with our parents or loved ones, which takes only 5 minutes but has a 5-hour impact!

Thirty minutes of physical activities like swimming, cardio, or any outdoor games-well, don't put the label of "I'm busy" on this again... A little bit of sunlight in the morning is essential for better sleep at night. A little time with our community, whether in the temple, church, gym, or just in our neighborhood...

These activities are just a few time-consuming ones, but in the long run, they act as a lubricant for your engine. Like a coolant that helps for a smooth run-it helps!!!

Tiny changes but remarkable results...

CHAPTER SIXTY-NINE

FRIENDSHIP

As an INFJ, I struggled to make friends because my combination of introversion and intuition made me very selective about my circle. However, I had a group of people I valued the most: my teachers, close friends, and relatives-essentially, "my people."

When we enter a new phase of life, we often lose touch with those from previous chapters. This is common. After graduation, how many of you still keep your high school friends in your circle? How many of your old friend groups are still active? How many of your old "gangs" are still a priority?

It's human nature. I was the same way. But I realized that if I continued this pattern throughout my journey, I would be alone forever. So, I decided to create a "good book," a list of people from my early days. I made an effort to call or message them once in a while.

As a result, I was able to make many genuine friends-fewer in quantity but greater in quality. However, I noticed that 95% of the time, I was the one who took the initiative. I was the one who started conversations and made the calls. Yes, it's necessary. If you want to maintain these connections, you need to make the effort. Nobody is going to come to you because everyone has their own priorities, hustles, and lives.

The best mantra is to "take initiative or to start."

The modern world faces a crisis of loneliness. Even though social media seems to make us more connected, it often makes us more isolated and less social.

Here's my formula:

1. Create a good book.
2. Start from your school days.
3. Take initiative to connect.
4. Prioritize...

It works!

CHAPTER SEVENTY

WHERE TO FIND YOUR WIFE...?

Recently, I watched a video titled "Where to Find Your Wife."
"A typical title," I thought.
Well, I'm still young, and I believe I'm not at the age for marriage, but out of curiosity, I watched the full-length video in one stretch. I also read a book that was recommended by that YouTuber. This guy had a far different approach to the idea of dating.
The lessons were:
1. Choose a woman who is equal and opposite to your polarity. There exist two different poles in sex: masculine and feminine.
The masculine one is the one who takes risks, responsibilities, makes decisions, and leads, while the feminine energy is full of love, care, and togetherness. He advised identifying your own traits, meaning how masculine or feminine you are. There is no one in this world who is fully feminine or fully masculine. Not every man is masculine, and not every woman is feminine; it changes according to the character of each person. Many

women possess masculine qualities, and many possess feminine traits too. So, know yourself and choose the opposite. If you are more masculine, choose a highly feminine one, and vice-versa.

2. He spoke about cold and hot nature in polarity, about sex, and about raising a family.

But in the end, there was an advice that opened my eyes, which was a warning sign to men:

"If you are looking for a long-term relationship or becoming a father, choose a woman who is going to raise your children, the one who possesses the qualities of a mother."

Damn...

Because our parents have sacrificed many things for our well-being. They struggled to provide a better education, food and accommodation, knowledge and wisdom, kindness and character because, for them, we are their world. What if I become a father? Definitely, I'm going to do the same, or work even harder than my parents did to make the best world for my next generation, and the quality of my partner is going to play a huge role in that. Well, she will be the one who is going to play a major role in their character development.

And he ended with a question:

"Do you date a woman who goes to clubs every night, drinks a lot, shows her butt on Instagram, or the one who has the qualities of a mother, a caretaker, a feminine woman?"

CHAPTER SEVENTY-ONE

MAKE TEXTING YOUR LAST PRIORITY

There are so many social media and connection platforms that claim to improve our social connections. But do they really enhance our social skills or deepen our relationships? I think not.

They have created a culture centered around texting. When I was dealing with a severe injury to my right leg ligament and was confined to bed for weeks, unable to walk or even stand up straight, I spent most of my days just staring at the ceiling fan in my room or looking out the window. During that time, many of the people who mattered most to me visited and spent time with me. They told me jokes, shared laughter, and we had some wonderful moments. Some friends called to check on me and see how I was doing.

But a few people, who I thought were close, just texted. I understand that not everyone can visit. Everyone is busy and has their own lives.

However, the people who truly cared made time for me, even on their busiest days.

Those who love us will be there for us, no matter how busy they are.

Would you go to work on a day when your child is undergoing surgery, even if your schedule is packed? Would you sleep soundly if your partner hadn't come home yet? Would you attend a cricket match if your mother was sick at home?

Most probably not-if you genuinely care.

So, if you truly like someone and want them in your circle, visit them. Have a real conversation. Don't hide behind "I'm busy." Just be honest and say they're not your priority.

If it's hard to visit, at least make a phone call. Listen to their voices and talk to them.

Make texting your last option for staying connected!

From my experience:

If someone invites me to an event via text, the chances of me attending are less than 10%.

If they call me, I'll mark it on my calendar.

If they invite me face-to-face by visiting my home, I'll get a fresh haircut, groom myself well, buy a gift, and be the first one to arrive.

I don't know if my way of measuring the genuineness of a bond is right or wrong, but it has helped me build a small circle of high-quality people.

If you truly need someone in your life, go to them, talk to them, and make texting your last option for connection. It takes time and effort, but it's how genuine bonds are formed. If it were easy, everyone would be doing it, right?

CHAPTER SEVENTY-TWO

Keeping The Consistency

Sticking to something consistently can be tough. During our film fest, my colleagues and I learned Surya Namaskar in different phases. I'm truly grateful to our mentor, Niyas Ram, for guiding us. But here's the catch-it was easy to learn, but hard to maintain. Consistency was the key, and I struggled

It was challenging at first, and I missed many days. But then, I discovered a simple yet powerful solution: I placed my yoga mat right in front of my bed. So every morning, the first thing I saw when I opened my eyes was my mat.

That became my ritual. It's been years now, and I haven't missed a single day!

The secret? It only took 2 minutes to put my mat on the floor. If I had focused on the entire Surya Namaskar session, I might have skipped it. But those first 2 minutes set the tone. Open my eyes, grab the mat, and boom-I had no choice but to get started. No more excuses.

We're all human. Even with discipline, the temptation to skip can be strong. Our "monkey brain" often tries to stop us from taking action. That's when we need to hack our surroundings to work in our favor.

Want to drink more water? Place a bottle in every corner of your house, and you'll find yourself reaching for it naturally. Want to read more? Leave a book on your bed, and you'll likely read a few pages before sleep.

It's not about to-do lists or phone reminders. The real game- changer is designing your environment to make good habits unavoidable.

CHAPTER SEVENTY-THREE

OUT WORK THEM ALL

You know what's the most painful feeling at the start of any journey? It's not the struggle, not the sacrifice - it's the criticism from others. Oh, they're always there, ready with their expert opinions.

Them: "Pffft, you're never going to do it. I told you..."

And so, you put in months of hard work. Blood, sweat, tears... and maybe a few energy drinks. But still, you haven't hit that big, shiny goal yet.

Them again: "See? I told you, you're not going to make it!"

And now you're starting to wonder... "Are they right?" You feel that sting because they're measuring in months.

But you keep pushing forward, determined, focused, and slightly caffeinated. A year goes by. A whole year! And guess what? Things still haven't clicked.

Them (who have never left, apparently): "Look, look! A whole year and still no results, huh? What did we say? We were right all along!"

And now, they're measuring in years...

And once more, you start to doubt. "Maybe they're right..."

But here's the kicker. They've been wrong the whole time! You see, they're measuring in days, weeks, and years... but you? You're measuring in decades. You're playing the long game, and they're looking for instant noodles.

So, let them count their days and tally their months. Because while they're busy measuring, you're busy building. And one day, when that decade rolls around, they'll wonder how you did it... and you'll just smile and say, "I told you so."

CHAPTER SEVENTY-FOUR

HAPPENS OVER TIME.....

Mammootty acted in over 400 films, but only around 50 were major commercial hits Yet, he's still one of the most respected, consistent, and celebrated actorsnafter 5 decades

Warren Buffett invested in hundreds of stocks, but built the majority of his wealth from just 10 of them and most of that came after his 60th birthday

It's not about instant success.

It's about consistency, patience and the power of compounding

Success rarely comes from one shot - it comes from showing up, over and over again, improving, failing, learning, and staying in the game long enough for the odds to turn in your favor.

There's no such thing as overnight success only long-term effort that becomes visible overnight.

CHAPTER SEVENTY-FIVE

DEAR INFJ ME....

From a young age, I've always struggled with social gatherings. These situations never felt natural or enjoyable to me, especially at events like marriage functions. I often found myself feeling bored, disconnected, and out of place. Wearing outfits that didn't match the climate, plastering on a fake smile for hours, and posing for photos with people who barely knew my name all felt meaningless and exhausting. On top of that, the food at these events was rarely to my liking, and I would always arrive late, only to find myself counting down the minutes until I could leave. This wasn't just a one-off experience; it happened repeatedly across various occasions.

As time went on, my family grew increasingly concerned about this aspect of my personality. They worried about how my reluctance to socialize would be perceived by relatives and friends. Often, they found themselves making excuses for me, trying to cover up my disinterest and disengagement, just to avoid embarrassment in front of others.

When faced with choices like:
1. Going shopping with friends

or

2. Staying at home and immersing myself in a good book

I almost always chose the second option. The idea of spending time in a crowded mall with a group of people was not appealing to me. If I absolutely had to go shopping, I preferred to go alone. I found solace in doing things independently-whether it was traveling, shopping, or even going to the movies. These solitary activities gave me a sense of freedom and peace that social gatherings never could. However, deep down, I knew that if I continued isolating myself, it could eventually take a toll on my mental health. After all, human beings are inherently social creatures. We thrive in connection with others, even if we don't crave constant interaction.

It became clear to me that while I didn't need people around all the time, I still needed some form of social engagement. Once a week, at least, was necessary to maintain a healthy balance. But despite this understanding, the pressure from those around me-friends, family, and society in general-to "fix" my introverted nature was overwhelming. They encouraged me to be more extroverted, to overcome my introversion, and to embrace the outgoing, social personality they believed I needed.

So, I tried. I pushed myself into social situations, attempting to play the part of the extrovert. But every time, it felt like I was wearing a mask. The more I pretended, the more disconnected and unsatisfied I felt. No matter how much I tried, being extroverted didn't come naturally to me, and it left me feeling drained and inauthentic. Eventually, I made a decision: instead of forcing myself to be someone I'm not, I would prioritize myself and my well-being.

A few years later, I took a personality test, and that experience brought so much clarity to my life. It helped me understand the way I am wired, and why I struggled with certain aspects of social interaction. The test confirmed that I am introverted, and it allowed me to embrace that part of myself rather than viewing it as something that needed to be changed. I realized that my introversion wasn't a flaw; it was simply part of who I am. With this new understanding. I made a crucial decision: to stay true to who I am and live life in a way That feels right to me. But at the same time, I also recognized the importance of socializing in moderation. While solitude is essential for recharging my energy.

I now know that occasional social interactions are necessary to maintain my mental and emotional health. It's about finding that balance -engaging with others on my terms, without sacrificing my need for personal space.

For anyone out there who is struggling with their introversion, let me offer this reassurance: being Introvertedness is not a limitation. In fact, introverts often have fewer, but much more meaningful connections.

We tend to be more introspective, disciplined, and thoughtful, and these qualities allow us to lead lives that are rich with depth and purpose. Our ability to reflect, create, and focus is a strength, not a weakness.

Yes, it's true that our path may be more challenging, especially in a world that seems to value extroversion. But in the end, the quality of our relationships, our self-awareness, and the fulfillment

We find meaningful pursuits that make our lives all the more rewarding.

CHAPTER SEVENTY-SIX

MODERN DATING

The problem with modern dating is this: People value others more than they value themselves.

They try so hard to be loved... That they forget to love themselves first.

You've heard this before, but it's true Fill your own glass before pouring into someone else's.

But what happens today? People abandon their habits... Ignore their routines... Lose their discipline... All just to keep someone else happy.

And then what? They end up alone. Confused. Burned out. Ask yourself honestly:

"Do you like that person?" - Yes.

"Do you like yourself when you're with them?" - No.

And that... is the real tragedy.

CHAPTER SEVENTY-SEVEN

STOP BEING A NERD

Rather than showcasing a seemingly perfect life on Instagram, focus on genuinely living a better life offline.

Today, many of us treat our Instagram accounts as personal portfolios, showcasing how incredible our lives appear in terms of friendships, relationships, fitness, and more. We often care more about curating a flawless online image than we do about cultivating a fulfilling real-life experience.

People design their media profiles more carefully than they design their actual lives.

However, those who truly lead remarkable lives seldom feel the need to broadcast it. For instance, Oscar-winning actor Cillian Murphy doesn't even have a social media account. Elon Musk, despite his online presence, reportedly has a screen time of less than 30 minutes a day. High performers like Cristiano Ronaldo didn't build their careers by first gaining followers on social media-he focused on football, and his success naturally drew fans. These individuals are immersed in their purpose, spending time with family and friends, and working hard to improve their lives. They're not concerned about the filters or background music in their pictures. In fact, most of their media content is handled by professionals specializing in marketing.

But these are the stories of high achievers. What about the average person?

Many consume social media obsessively, thinking that frequent posts, perfect filters, and more likes equate to a better life. The truth is, they're wasting hours on media that adds no real value

By the end of the day, their brains are exhausted from screen time and constant comparisons.

So, what's the remedy?

Get more social-in real life.

Start by getting sunlight first thing in the morning, instead of immediately checking your phone. Talk with people in your neighborhood. Join a local library or club and engage with others. Visit a nearby temple in the evenings to find a sense of peace. Get involved in outdoor activities like swimming, walking, or cycling.

By doing this, you'll feel a natural surge of dopamine-a sense of calm and mindfulness that social media once disrupted.

Just put that smartphone in the corner of your room and start living a life in the real world.

CHAPTER SEVENTY-EIGHT

LIVE YOUR TRUTH

Stop Over-Explaining Yourself

Most of us have this habit we feel the need to explain everything about the decisions we make.
Your heart tells you: "End the friendship." But your mind jumps in: "She did this... he didn't do that... they said this..." And you spiral into a sea of justifications.

Let's be honest - that's just mental masturbation.
Instead, say this to yourself with clarity and courage: "I don't value that friendship anymore. So, I'm walking away. End of story."

But here's the problem we often dive into an ocean of reasons just to justify our actions. "I quit because I didn't like it." "I rejected it because it didn't feel right."
Simple. Direct. Honest.

Only a few people have the guts to say that. Why? Because deep down, we feel like we'll have to justify our decisions to society someday as if we're in a constant courtroom

defending our emotions.
But the truth is: No one really cares why you feel what you feel.
So stop explaining.

Live your truth.
Close the chapter without footnotes.

CHAPTER SEVENTY-NINE

THE ENEMIES

"Well, I don't want to be hated, I don't need enemies..." ~ pfff

If you have good values, passion, vision, morals, and a keen, sharp attitude, I don't know whether you'll become successful, but you will certainly get one thing-enemies.

If you don't have any, it means...

1. You're a nice guy.
2. You have a weak character.
3. You shift your opinion according to people and circumstances (simply put, you lack a spine).
4. You're a people-pleaser.
5. You care more about external validation than your inner self.
6. You don't respect yourself at all.

If you're strong, there will be many who become jealous of your progress. Many will try to prove you wrong, some will pray for your defeat, and others will laugh at you.

According to Robert Greene: "Having enemies is a sign of power."

If you don't have any enemies, it means you're doing something boring and playing the role of the "good boy."

Mahatma Gandhi, Leo Messi, Jesus Christ, Lord Krishna, Nikola Tesla... and the list of these giants has one thing in common-they had haters.

If you are someone who wants to make a change and has a keen vision, the first door you have to face is hate-it's common. But the funniest part is that someone who was an enemy at one stage often becomes a friend later. I've experienced this many times. The psychology is that most enemies don't want to destroy us; they want to prove something in a healthy way.

That's why we see many entrepreneurs progressing in business with their previous enemies. So many athletes win medals with the help of their former opponents. Many kings, artists, and scientists have made revolutionary changes by working with their past rivals.

So, if you have an enemy, just wait. Look five years down the road, and see if this happens in your life too

CHAPTER EIGHTY

ACTION AND INTENTION

An action can be judged as good or bad based on the intention behind it.
Harming someone may generally seem wrong but if you harm a terrorist to protect an innocent child, the action becomes justified.
It is the intention behind the action that defines its moral value

CHAPTER EIGHTY-ONE

NECESSITY...

Consider two situations:
1: I like Lamborghini. I wish I had one...
2: My right leg aches, I can't move it, I need to fix it...
The first one is a desire, and the second one is a necessity.

Well, we can travel in a Honda, right? So do we need a Lamborghini for that? No, it's not necessary to own a Lamborghini. But what about your right leg? It's a necessary one-you need to fix it, or else you will suffer. It's a necessity to fix it. You will do whatever it takes-meet surgeons, take loans, keep up with the medicines and support until it gets better-and finally, you fix it. You don't even care about the money, time, or anything else because it is your necessity. What about the Lamborghini? It was just a desire, right? Well, we all have desires-about our career, health, family, and so on. But only a few people achieve them. We may think of them as the lucky ones.

A few days ago, I watched the A.R.M movie, where a young boy who was playing volleyball at Irinjalakuda was performing so well...

Was it just his desire to become an actor?

Look at any high-performing individuals in sports, arts, or literature. It was not only desire; perhaps they had a special type of desire known as a "burning desire" or a necessity.

Their desire became a necessity, so they achieved it. If it becomes your necessity, you will sacrifice anything for it, go miles, risk everything for it...

So, the label of desire is not enough to get it, and the charisma of luck doesn't even exist. What matters is your necessity.

If it was just your desire, you'd still be driving a Honda and wishing for a Lamborghini. But if it was your necessity, you'd already be in a Lamborghini!

CHAPTER EIGHTY-TWO

HAPPINESS FOR SALE

Is it hard to be happy?
I believe there are practices that can keep us happy, mainly by sustaining the dopamine levels in our brains.
These include:
1. Gratitude
2. Quality Relationships
3. Purpose

Gratitude: Adopting the mindset of "I'm grateful for what I have right now" is a powerful practice. Personally, I strive to improve in all aspects of life- professionally, with family, in fitness-but I always maintain gratitude for what I have while working toward more.

Often, we're unaware of the blessings we already possess, instead focusing on our struggles or blaming others. But somewhere, someone else is praying for the life we have. If you've graduated and are struggling to find a job, remember there are many who haven't even cleared their courses. Be grateful and keep trying.

If you're feeling low, think of those battling cancer in a hospital who wish they had the life and health you have now. The mindset of "I'm grateful for what I have, but I strive for more" is one of the best feelings to cultivate.

Quality Relationships: In my view, it's not about how many friends you have, but the quality of those relationships. It takes years to build strong bonds, and it's that compassion and trust between people that matters. You may have had lots of friends in school or college, but quality is defined by the depth and longevity of those connections.

In today's generation, quality friendships are harder to maintain. Less is more -keep your circle small but meaningful. A tight-knit group where you can find support and healing when you're down is invaluable. Many Gen Zers struggle with lasting relationships, so keep a good book as a companion and prioritize what truly matters. It works!

Purpose: This is the pillar that holds everything together-the meaning of life. Ask yourself: Why am I living? or What would I do for the rest of my life if I had already achieved all my success? The answer is your purpose, your Ikigai. It's the thing that drives you to get out of bed in the morning, that challenges you daily, and fulfills you as you pursue it.

Purpose gives us so much more than a 9-to-5 job ever could. It enhances the quality of life, enriches your connections, and gives you a vision for the future.

CHAPTER EIGHTY-THREE

Stoicism And Ryan Holiday

The best two things I started following are Stoicism and Ryan Holiday.

1. Stoicism is an ancient Greek philosophy founded in the early 3rd century BC. It teaches that the path to a good life is found in accepting the present moment as it is, focusing on what we can control, and cultivating virtues such as wisdom, courage, justice, and temperance. Stoics believe that external events are beyond our control, but our reactions and attitudes toward them are within our power.

2. Ryan Holiday is a modern author, marketer, and entrepreneur best known for popularizing Stoic philosophy in contemporary times. His books, including
The Obstacle Is the Way, Ego Is the Enemy, and Discipline Is Destiny, draw on ancient Stoic teachings and apply them to modern life, focusing on self-discipline, resilience, and personal growth.

If you want to learn some basics, just Google this

man's name or search in an online bookstore. You'll find
a bunch of books-grab one and practice the techniques. While I'm a beginner in Stoicism, I assure you of one thing: it is a step toward knowledge and wisdom, and you won't see the world the same way again. You'll notice tiny but remarkable changes in all areas of your life!

CHAPTER EIGHTY-FOUR

How to Win In Public Speaking

Public speaking is an art. To express what's on our minds in front of an audience takes a lot of courage. It is not easy, but you can master it.

1. Make Bullet Points

Before a speech, write a script and practice it in private. Practice more, but don't memorize it word-for-word. Instead, make bullet points from the script and focus on remembering those key points. Deliver your speech based on them.

2. Speak Less Than Necessary

If you speak too much, there is a chance you might say something foolish. Keep it concise because one drop of poison is enough to turn a delicious pudding into a sour one.

3. Speak Slowly

Stay calm and patient while delivering your speech. Anxiety often makes us speak faster. Practice this: take a double inhale and a deep exhale before starting. This helps reduce stress.

4. Control Your Voice

Make enough pauses. Use full stops, exclamations, and adjust your tone according to the emotion you wish to convey. If your topic involves love, fear, or surprise, let the audience feel it.

Explain your points like a story, creating emotional attachment with your voice.

Public speaking is a key pillar of power-an essential tool for persuasion. Great leaders like Hitler and Mao were effective speakers. In fact, their words were their tools for mastery.

CHAPTER EIGHTY-FIVE

STRESS AND PRESSURE..

A little bit of stress and pressure is good for your drive. Thomas Edison made a remarkable statement before he invented the electric bulb during a press meet, saying, "I will light up New York City within 5 years." Everyone was at their peak of curiosity because, until then, they had been using many other methods for lighting, which were dangerous and expensive. However, Edison's labmates weren't happy with that statement because they doubted whether it was possible within 5 years.

But they took it as a challenge! They felt a little bit of pressure to keep that public promise. They worked hard, and their expectations became a reality. They succeeded in lighting up the entire city within 5 years!

In order to get things done, we have to set a deadline first, or else we will keep moving our goalposts. Set a deadline that makes your work challenging and creates a little stress in your mind, making you wonder whether it can be completed. That stress and pressure drive you toward completion.

But never set an impossible goal or deadline. Just as Edison didn't claim, "I will light up the entire world in 5 years," he focused on New York City.. not the entire world

CHAPTER EIGHTY-SIX

THE CHAD

You may see some men who are good in their looks, studies, extracurricular activities, fitness, relationships, and in all areas of their life.

How do they achieve this?

It's because of their high stress tolerance.

They care about all the mentioned areas with equal importance. They know it's not just one thing, one material, or one achievement that defines success. There are people who win an Oscar but fail in their family life, or earn millions but fail in their fitness.

To master all aspects of life, we need a high level of stress tolerance. It is stressful to have a kind conversation with our kids after a terrible meeting with clients; it is stressful to go to the temple after hitting leg day.

But they understand that it's essential. That's how they master their minds.

They train themselves to deal with it. They know it is going to be painful, but it is necessary.

CHAPTER EIGHTY-SEVEN

GURUDWARA

Just before the winter of 2023, I visited Jalandhar Cantonment for the first time. The military zone.... The giant tanks, weapons, and the officers-whoa! That was quite a moment!

During the return journey, I was feeling cold and had a fever, and my return ticket wasn't confirmed yet. So, I had to stay somewhere, but I never had enough money to get a hotel. I was tired and exhausted in search of a bed to sleep. I ended up in a temple that they call the Gurudhwara. In the Gurudhwara, if you pay 100 rupees, you can stay there and get free food too!

It was a lottery for me, and I rushed to the Gurudwara and registered my name. A Sikh brother in a blue kurta and pajama arranged a bed for me. It was a dormitory with clean and neat bathroom facilities. I had a sleep, and when I woke up, I heard the song from the temple. One elder Sikh brother asked me to take a shower and come to the temple. That man had a one-foot-length white beard and was holding several types of knives along with his dress. He was carrying many more items, like a belt full of bells, heavy shoes, and different Sikh traditional ornaments. When I got into the temple, they gave me a shawl to tie on my head. I just sat on the ground along with other Sikh brothers. No chanting, no mantras, no other noise... a true calmness.

Till the end of that day, I never touched my phone. I spent my entire day in that Gurudwara, without any distractions from the outside world, ate langar food, and spent much time in their garden... and felt one thing: peace.

In this world of rush, we often run behind the unwanted-money, status, power. We consider these as happiness, the achievements as success, and the drive as pleasure. But the Gurudwara taught me one thing: peace is more important than happiness.

Imagine you are at your deathbed; you will be looking for your loved ones rather than the medals you got because it is rooted in your inner calmness. You feel at peace when they are with you.

And the Gurudwara brought my favorite person to my side, which was the happiest version of me.

When I left the Gurudwara, I hugged all my Sikh brothers, said goodbye, and wished I could have spent one more day there.

If you ever visit Punjab, just go to a nearby Gurudwara and spend at least two days there. You can find one thing: your best version!

CHAPTER EIGHTY-EIGHT

How To Groom Well

It is necessary to keep a sharp look. As a man, it is essential! But how do you maintain it? Here are some tips:

1. Workout

Lifting weights is an essential tool to look good, especially for the upper body. Focus on building an aesthetic or "V" shaped body so that you look attractive in all types of clothing. A bulky chest, strong neck, shoulders, and well-defined abs can enhance your appearance. Cardio helps reduce fat on your facial muscles, which highlights your cheekbones and jawline.

2. Find Your Grooming Style

Determine your face shape and select a grooming style accordingly. Many guides are available online to help you find your face shape. Follow the styles that suit you. It's advisable to get a grooming cut once every 4 weeks.

3. Practice Mindfulness

Your face is a reflection of your soul, so purify it. Practice yoga and meditation daily to boost positive energy within you, which eventually reflects on your face. A pleasant and positive energy in your body is essential.

Good sleep also enhances these benefits, as sleep is another form of meditation.

4. Keep a Morning Routine

Get at least 7 hours of sleep, expose yourself to 2 minutes of sunlight within the first 30 minutes of waking up, and drink plenty of water. If possible, go for a morning walk.

5. Follow the Micros

Body:Clean diet, cold showers, good quality products

Mind: Less screen time, good quality relationships, journaling.

Looks are a combination of many factors: body, dressing, mind, habits, and diet. While a makeover kit may offer instant changes, for the long term, you must sharpen the roots and that always takes time!

CHAPTER EIGHTY-NINE

CLEAN THEM UP...

How to Keep Your Room Clean and Neat??
Buy a new waste bin and place it in the corner of your room. Our brain has a tendency to use new things more often.
Why do we use a waste bin? To clean or put away the waste, right?
Eventually, your room will stay clean!

CHAPTER NINETY

Fix Your Roots

Every problem has a solution...
You are overweight; you went to the gym, hit the workout session.
But was it the junk food and sugar you consumed that were the main reasons for it?
You feel stressed, follow some yoga practices, practice meditation, and mindfulness.
But was it your improper sleep and excessive screen time that caused the stress?
You had another breakup... You spent some time with friends and later started dating someone new.
But was it your past traumas that failed you in each relationship?
Well, every fever has paracetamol to heal! And every problem has a solution. But every problem has a cause too... So, fix the root first, then go to the stem!

CHAPTER NINETY-ONE

FAKE YOUR FEELINGS

You felt so ashamed while paying the bills because you didn't have enough money... And you decided to become a millionaire!

You felt insulted when somebody mocked you... And you decided to prove them wrong...

You failed in the exams... And decided to score an A+...

Months later, you are still struggling to make 1000 rupees, haven't made any progress, and still fail at exams...

Why?

It's because the decisions were based on your feelings, and feelings fade away-while you remain!

CHAPTER NINETY-TWO

POWER OF AUTHENTICITY

I think the most desired quality of a leader is "Authenticity."
The measure of how true you are to yourself!
Not only in leadership but in every area of life. How authentic are you? In your work? Family? Friendships and relationships?
Or are you the one who keeps them all for your own benefit? Just for money? Just for relaxation, fulfilling needs, sex?
Yes, you may earn instant benefits by doing the opposite, but in the long term, how true and genuine you are matters the most. Because in order to sustain something for over a decade, it needs strong roots, and that is "Trust."

CHAPTER NINETY-THREE

GO FOR ENGINEERING BABE...

If you ask someone who completed Engineering: "Should I send my kid to an Engineering college?" The most common answer will be "no." But for me, it's "yes." Why? Because we engineers are the ones who stay up-to-date with modern technology and use it productively. We go through a bulky syllabus, filled with a never-ending series of exams, assignments, labs, seminars, and projects. Yet, we are also the ones who enjoy life the most, especially in government colleges (none of our parents had any idea what we did in the hostels!). We participate in every activity and still manage to score an "S" in each subject. That's because we know how to deal with stress and get results.

And finally, we learn everything... except Engineering!

CHAPTER NINETY-FOUR

#Truth

"Find someone, solve each and every problem of that person.
Then,
you become their next problem!"

CHAPTER NINETY-FIVE

How to Sleep Well

Sleep is the foundation of our physical and mental health. In order to perform well, we have to maintain a sleep discipline.

1. Get Enough Morning Sunlight

Just after waking up in the morning, make sure you are getting enough sunlight in your eyes (avoid screens for 1 hour). Go for a walk for 10 minutes and ensure you have had enough sunlight; it keeps you refreshed and helps you achieve a good night's sleep.

2. Lower the Temperature

Just before sleeping, adjust the room or mattress temperature to 15-20°C. Lower temperatures are optimal for good quality sleep. That's why we struggle to get up in the monsoon season! If you live in a city like Chennai, make sure you have a good air conditioner in your room (or go to the terrace and sleep with fewer clothes).

3. Engage in Physical Activities

Exercise daily, especially in the morning. The more you engage in physical activities like weightlifting, cardio, and yoga, the better your quality of sleep will be. The more your body moves, the better the quality of sleep you get.

4. Adjust Your Screen Settings

Right now, I'm using a Galaxy A05, which has a wonderful grayscale. This is an optimal combination for our eyes. Alternatively, simply avoid screens during the night!

5. Get Enough Bedtime

To sleep for 7 hours, plan for at least 7.45 hours of bedtime!

CHAPTER NINETY-SIX

THE ART OF SAYING NO

If someone asked for a pen during our school days: "Hey Ajay, don't you have a black pen?"
And me: "I'm sorry, I don't have one. I only have a blue one."
What if I had just said: "Nope."
And later, in high school, when someone asked: "Are you coming for the Wonderla trip?"
And me: "I'm sorry, I'll catch a cold... and my body is already too weak... blah, blah, blah."
What if my reply had been: "No."
When that junior girl asked: "Can you wear that black kurta this weekend?"
And me: "Oh, it's at home. It's already taken for washing."
What if I had said: "No, not possible."
Is it necessary to explain the story behind your "No" to everyone?

CHAPTER NINETY-SEVEN

SCREEN TIME

Recently, I have reduced my screen time to 2 hours a day for a week.

Here are the tips that I used:

1. Using grayscale mode

We are in the age of attention-based income, where creators try to grab our attention at any cost by using highly saturated thumbnails, attractive app icons, and eye-catching visuals. The simplest and most attractive apps get used more than the average ones. Look at the app icons-they are ideally designed, and the color palettes they follow are too perfect. But what if we turn our screens to grayscale?

Try it once.

Have you ever opened YouTube in grayscale? It seems like an old movie theater. And Instagram? You have no idea how pathetic the curated reels and ads look. Eventually, your mind reduces exposure because it starts disliking the visuals. As a result, your screen time goes down.

2. Customize your notifications

Reality: you die in a car accident, but you still get enough emails from Spotify. Clean the mess-especially the notifications. We use hundreds of apps, newsletters, and our notification bars are sometimes flooded. Clean them up. Unsubscribe from the unwanted ones. Only keep the necessary email notifications and reminders. And finally, quit social media as soon as possible!

3. Spend your free time wisely

Most of my friends are always on their phones. So, I spend my free time with the elderly and the little ones. They need you sometimes to listen and sometimes to entertain. Whenever I spend time with kids, I feel like time flies. There's a little bit of chaos for sure-usual cries and complaints-but always free from the distractions of the external world!

CHAPTER NINETY-EIGHT

BE A STOIC

"The most formidable individuals are those who remain calm in every situation.
They stand still during arguments, speak sparingly, and rise above violence.
Often misunderstood as stubborn, they possess the virtue of patience.
It is easy to lash out, but the truly strong remain composed and avoid needless drama. Beware of them-while they may seem pleasant, composed, and indifferent, they can endure insults in silence, absorbing pain that slowly chips away at them. But they know precisely when and how to respond, with deliberate timing and precision.
They observe, analyze everything, adapt to changes, and make decisions with wisdom.
Remember: Never mistake their forgiveness for weakness, nor their restraint for foolishness. When they finally act, you will be unprepared for the weight of their response."
This version reflects the Stoic ideals of patience, composure, and the controlled use of power.

CHAPTER NINETY-NINE

DON'T MISS 2 DAYS...

It is harder to keep a habit in a row, even without missing a day. On that journey, it is common to skip a few days. If you are committed to going for a morning walk every day, it's normal to miss it on some days. After all, you can't go for a walk when you're suffering from a high fever, right?

For a special category of people often referred to as perfectionists, missing one day feels like a big mistake, which can lead to extreme burnout.

But it's okay to skip one day, because what matters is the compound effect. If you skipped a day, just look at how many days you've completed this month. If it's more than 25, hats off! There's no need to blame yourself for missing a few days - results accumulate through consistent action.

Remember: skipping one day is okay, but never miss two days in a row, because that could mark the beginning of a new habit!

~ credits: Atomic habits

CHAPTER ONE HUNDRED

EXPECTATIONS

You can disappoint people... even without doing anything wrong.
Why? One word: Expectations.

Sometimes, you give your best. You work with full heart and maximum effort. But your performance doesn't meet their standards, not because it's bad-But because it's less than what they expected.
And suddenly, you're seen as weak. You're labelled a failure. You're judged not by your intention or effort, but by how well you matched the mob's expectations.

Congratulations-now you're the most hated person in the room. Not because you were wrong. But because you didn't meet their idea of right.

CHAPTER ONE HUNDRED AND ONE

FEAR...

I think fear of failure plays an important role in all achievements.

Since my childhood, I have belonged to a category commonly termed as "Padippi"-the topper in exams, the class leader... medals and awards, etc.

During all exams, I had one predominant feeling: fear. The fear of scoring low. If you are a topper, then you have to keep that title. Getting the first position once is hard, but keeping it forever is even harder!

Once you score high, it becomes your responsibility to score high again. For example, if you get an A+ in one exam, you have to maintain it in your +2 exams as well, or else you are seen as a failure in the eyes of society.

The fear of losing the level I had reached was the real driving force. What if I lose that crown? What if I score low? That fear created enough stress. And stress is necessary for making progress.

In a podcast, Steven Bartlett commented that "In my locality, my house was the worst one to live in, and I feared I would die in the same conditions. That fear was the driving force that led to my first million." Now, he is a multimillionaire!

In every competitive exam and in the Olympics, the winners had one thing in common: the fear of failure.

The constant questioning of "What if I lose?" The shame and pain of losing is often more significant than the medals and glories. The fear of failure plays a bigger role than success stories because motivation doesn't last long, but pain does. And the pain of regret stays much longer.

CHAPTER ONE HUNDRED AND TWO

BULK IN RESULTS

"Results become only attractive when they are accumulated in large quantities.
A wider bicep, long beard, Oscars, Lambos on the porch get noticed first, right?"

CHAPTER ONE HUNDRED AND THREE

SIGNS OF POOR MENTAL HEALTH

1. You often scroll through social media even when there is nothing of interest, especially during work.
2. You depend on music to improve your mood and play it throughout your work time, at the gym, and wherever you go.
3. You can't sit alone or focus on anything for more than 7 minutes; you frequently shift tasks.
4. You are unable to properly read a paragraph from an email or book, rushing through only the key points or highlights.
5. You react to someone's arguments instead of checking the facts and responding accordingly.

Remedy: Fix yourself first!
Action: Meditate daily for at least 10 minutes.

CHAPTER ONE HUNDRED AND FOUR

Brain Health vs Mental Health

Brain Health vs Mental Health: What's the Difference?

Most people are familiar with the term mental health, but rarely do we hear about brain health. Are they the same? Not at all.

Think of it this way:
Brain health is like the hardware of a computer.
Mental health is like the software running on that hardware.

If the brain-the physical structure-is damaged or not functioning properly, it can directly impact our thoughts, emotions, and behavior. For example, studies show that people with anxiety often have structural changes in the amygdala, the part of the brain that processes fear and emotion.

This means that taking care of your brain is just as

important as taking care of your mental health. A damaged brain can lead to serious mental health issues. Just like in a computer, if the hardware is faulty, the software can crash-even if it's perfectly written.
So let's start paying attention to both: Protect your brain. Nourish your mind.

CHAPTER ONE HUNDRED AND FIVE

TRUTHS ABOUT THE RICH

1. More money doesn't make you rich, but more freedom does: Time freedom and location freedom are crucial in achieving financial freedom.
2. Money can buy you happiness...
3. Building a business may not lead you to wealth, but it will give you stress.
4. Savings and 9-5 jobs don't make you rich.
5. You become rich when you stop giving a fu*k about your wallet.
6. Rich = mission + money + progress + friends + family + love + physical health + mental health + joy.

CHAPTER ONE HUNDRED AND SIX

DEAR PROVIDERS

Be careful while providing these...! Help, support, love, care, money...

There was a hotel owner. One day, a beggar came to him and begged for food, and out of sympathy, he gave him a full meal for free. A week later, the beggar came again, and the hotel owner did the same. The beggar was happy, and this repeated for weeks. Then, once the hotel owner gave him only tea and a snack instead of a full meal and did the same for the next few weeks. The beggar, however, wasn't satisfied and eventually asked, 'Only snacks... huh?'

The hotel owner was shocked by the word 'only!'

Yes, this happens. If you are the one who gives candy to a child all the time, it doesn't matter how many times you've given it. But it matters when you stop-the child will be upset, saying, 'No candy today?'

You donated your eyes, huh! Well, next time, they'll wait for your head, not just your eyebrows...

It is human nature today.

You may receive blessings while providing, but if you stop, you'll get something else for sure: a little bit of resentment.

Once you start providing something, you have to maintain that level... otherwise, you may end up being seen as a villain forever."

CHAPTER ONE HUNDRED AND SEVEN

FEATURES

Since my teenage years, I have been interested in using smartwatches. You can call, listen to music, measure heartbeats, and track your phone with them.

But when I finally got one, I used it for only one purpose: checking the time. The features were impressive, but I never needed them. Why should I check my blood pressure often? I'm not a physician, right?

Whenever I looked at my smartwatch screen, I felt only one thing-abundance. A lot of icons and options; most were useful but unnecessary.

So, I went back to my analog watch. The one with a navy-blue strap and a golden outline. It only had one thing to offer: the time. And that was all I needed.

Sometimes,
Too many features = use of no features

CHAPTER ONE HUNDRED AND EIGHT

ART OF STAYING HARD

We all can perform when we have enough love, support, energy, and a clear mind to make progress.

It's common, but what we do at our lowest matters the most. Many give up, turn their backs, or quit.

But the wise realize that this feeling will pass. These emotions aren't permanent. Sometimes, we feel joy, and sometimes, we feel pain.

Can we keep our heads up at our lowest? That's what matters most.

Can we still perform when we're alone, afraid, and tired?

To do so, we have to conquer ourselves, and that comes from discipline-taking action when we don't feel like it.

Some always wait for the perfect time to act, but discipline teaches us that the act itself is the perfect time.

CHAPTER ONE HUNDRED AND NINE

BEWARE THIS MADNESS

In my neighborhood, there is a man who always drinks a lot and causes trouble all around our area, especially during the night. But ever since Rajuettan, who served in the Indian Army for years, built a new home in our locality, that drunk guy has never caused any violence. The idea is simple-if he tries it again, he'll be taken care of with serious consequences.

There was also a bisexual man at my work who was a constant problem for me. Inappropriate touching was the worst issue I faced from him, and he often engaged in explicit conversations. Initially, I tried to avoid him; every time he approached, I would walk away. Then one day, out of anger and frustration, I told him, "Take your hands off, or I'll cut your balls off, you c*nt!"

He never approached me again, and I was finally free.

The same thing happened when I returned from Chennai. A guy in my village asked me about a fluid mechanics theorem, and I helped clarify his doubts. But he kept asking the same question week after week. One day, when I was sleeping, he came to my home with the same question again. I was so irritated! I barely socialize, but wherever I go, this guy finds a way to ruin my day with hours of unwanted talk.

I told my family about it.

- "Hey Ajay, just ignore him. He's just a freak," they said.

Then one day, I finally told him, "Just f**k off. I have other things to do."

In all three cases, the idea of ignoring them didn't work; they needed some form of fear to stop their nasty actions. Some people label others as "weak," "drunk," or "freaks" to humiliate them. But have you ever heard of a drunk guy attacking a police or military officer? They know the consequences would be severe.

Forgiving and ignoring are good virtues, but sometimes they can be self-destructive. Forgive mistakes, but not actions done intentionally. For some people, it's just fun-a way to pass time-but don't let your empathy lead to your own suffering. Set a deadline for all the nonsense. Sometimes a firm response in necessary situations saves us.

CHAPTER ONE HUNDRED AND TEN

KEEP SOME BOUNDARIES

In this era of instant pleasures, people are chasing foolishness. The obsession with showboating, especially on social media, has become a real threat. People tend to project a perfect life rather than actually living one.
Queen Elizabeth never spoke to a reporter on record, and George Washington was famously strict about his privacy. Yet today, many idolize reality stars, YouTubers, and influencers who "spill everything" in front of a camera. But they aren't gods-they're just seeking attention.
The happiest people don't feel the need to show off.
They're too busy actually living their lives.
So before you start crafting a personal portfolio on Instagram, ask yourself: Who do you care about more-you or how others perceive you?
This is why, today, people bring their cameras to the gym more often than their towels, and they spend more on materials, clothes, and cosmetics than on books.
You don't have to broadcast every trip, tea time, movie night, or personal moment.

Just be a mature person in a world full of emotionally immature children.

CHAPTER ONE HUNDRED AND ELEVEN

STOP THIS BULLSHIT

Just because you felt sadness doesn't mean you're at the stage of depression.

Just because someone shouted at you in public doesn't mean that person has borderline disorder.

If someone forgot their keys, that doesn't label them as having ADHD.

Years ago, these words were so rare. But as the media began to infiltrate our minds, some influencers and attention-seekers started using these terms often to gain views, leading consumers to believe everything they say without question.

Poor sleep, excessive screen time, or the type of content you consume can also impact our behavior. Music, movies, ads—they're all changing the brains of Gen Z, shaping behavior in subtle ways, often in ways that don't serve them well.

Reminder: Just because your son vomited in the morning doesn't mean he's pregnant. Maybe it's last night's vodka causing the trouble.

After Word

I'm a poor writer but a terrible reader... I quit reading the Geeta during my school days and restarted at the age of 21. By 2024, I had read the Geeta three times, along with books by authors like Ryan Holiday, Robert Greene, and Mark Manson, all of whom became part of my reading list. These influences became the root of this book, which took over six months to complete. Initially, it was never meant to become a book... but today, as I complete it, I can proudly say that I am now a better reader—a habit I once disliked.

The best tools that helped me complete this book were reading, listening, and journaling. I feel each and every page of this book; in many ways, I have lived this book.

After starting Tink Talks, which became the foundation of this book, I noticed meaningful changes in the people around me:

- Two of my friends and one of my cousins started going to the gym.
- My family members began reading books.
- My old school friends and teachers are now in my close friends group.
- One of my old college mates started writing.
- One of my seniors began guided meditation, and another started journaling.
- A friend of mine began reducing his screen time.
- Another friend started reading Ryan Holiday's books.

Well, if somebody says you can't change the world, my answer is:

"Yes, you can. First, be the change you want to see in others!"

Tink Talks

Tink talks is my daily journal which I used to share through my Instagram stories daily.. . This book is the collection of Tink talks which I started in June 2024. After starting T.T I was able to connect with many of my old friends, teachers and I used to discuss with my friends for a few minutes about the topic of each day... The topics that I share include my thoughts, quotes from my favorite books, Podcasts and lessons that I gained from my own experiences.

You can also check in the upcoming episodes of Tink talks on Instagram @Ajaynath.r and can share your thoughts and comments though your messages or can head to

Email: ajaynathtr373@gmail.com.

My Reading List

Before writing anything in this book, I was in a terrible period where I spent more time with books than with my friends and parents. And I think reading is the best habit that I have developed in the past few years. Here, I'm attaching my favorite books that you can also refer to

Atomic habits by James clear

Atomic habits is the Bible for developing good habits and removing the bad ones. Atomic Habits by James Clear is a popular self-help book that focuses on building effective habits and breaking unproductive ones. Clear introduces a simple yet powerful framework for habit formation, emphasizing that small, incremental changes (or "atomic" habits) can lead to remarkable results over time. The book's core idea is that by improving just 1% each day, one can make significant progress toward goals.Clear breaks down habits into four parts: cue, craving, response, and reward.

The way of the superior man by David Deida

The Way of the Superior Man by David Deida is a guide to living a life of purpose, authenticity, and deep personal growth. The book explores the dynamics of masculinity, relationships, and spiritual development, offering insights on how men can navigate their personal and professional lives with greater clarity and strength.Deida discusses the concept of the "superior man," someone who lives with a clear sense of purpose, embraces his masculine energy, and remains deeply connected to his inner self.

Ego is the Enemy by Ryan holiday

Ego is the Enemy by Ryan Holiday is a book that explores how the ego—our inflated sense of self-importance—can hinder personal growth, success, and happiness. Drawing on historical examples, philosophy, and psychology, Holiday argues that ego is a major barrier to achieving greatness, building strong relationships, and navigating challenges.The book is divided into three parts: Aspire, Success, and Failure. Each section highlights how ego manifests in different stages of life and how it can sabotage progress.

Geeta by Vedha Vyasa

The Bhagavad Gita, often referred to simply as the Gita, is a 700-verse Hindu scripture that is part of the ancient Indian epic, the Mahabharata. Written by the sage Vyasa, it presents a profound conversation between Prince Arjuna and Lord Krishna on the battlefield of Kurukshetra. Facing a moral dilemma about fighting in the war, Arjuna is filled with doubt and sorrow, questioning the righteousness of battle and the responsibilities it imposes.

Krishna, serving as Arjuna's charioteer and guide, imparts timeless spiritual wisdom, covering themes like duty, righteousness, devotion, and self-realization. The dialogue is organized into 18 chapters, each exploring different paths to spiritual growth, including the paths of devotion (bhakti), knowledge (jnana), and action (karma). Krishna explains the concept of dharma (duty) and encourages Arjuna to rise above personal attachments, showing him that true wisdom lies in detachment and seeing beyond the dualities of life.

The Gita addresses universal questions about purpose, the nature of the self, and the path to liberation (moksha), making it one of the most influential texts in philosophy and spirituality. Its teachings have been studied and revered worldwide, offering guidance for living a life of integrity, courage, and self-mastery.

IKIGAI by Héctor García and Francesc Miralles

Ikigai: The Japanese Secret to a Long and Happy Life by Héctor García and Francesc Miralles explores the Japanese concept of ikigai, which translates roughly to "a reason for being" or "a reason to wake up in the morning." The book delves into how finding and pursuing one's ikigai — a balance between passion, mission, vocation, and profession — can lead to a life of purpose, satisfaction, and longevity.Drawing on research and interviews with residents of Okinawa, Japan, known for its high population of centenarians, the authors share insights into how lifestyle, community, diet, and mindfulness contribute to both happiness and health.

The subtle art of not giving a Fck by Mark Manson*

The Subtle Art of Not Giving a Fck* by Mark Manson is a self-help book that challenges traditional positive-thinking approaches to personal growth and happiness. Instead of promoting relentless optimism, Manson argues that life is full of struggles and that accepting limitations, flaws, and negative experiences can lead to more genuine fulfillment.

The book encourages readers to be selective about what they care deeply about, suggesting that most things are not worth stressing over. Manson advocates for embracing life's hardships, facing painful truths, and focusing on values that genuinely matter, rather than chasing superficial goals like fame or wealth.

48 laws of power by Robert Greene

The 48 Laws of Power by Robert Greene is a bestselling book that explores strategies for gaining and maintaining power in social, professional, and political situations. Drawing from historical examples, philosophical insights, and the lives of influential figures, Greene outlines 48 specific "laws" or principles that individuals can use to navigate complex power dynamics.

The laws cover various tactics, from cultivating mystery and controlling one's emotions to knowing when to assert dominance and when to remain silent. Each chapter explains a different law, its benefits, and potential pitfalls, with real-life stories illustrating how it has been applied (or violated) by notable figures like Napoleon, Machiavelli, and Cleopatra.

Meditations by Marcus Aurelius

Meditations by Marcus Aurelius is a collection of personal writings by the Roman Emperor, originally intended as private reflections. The book is considered one of the greatest works of Stoic philosophy, offering timeless insights into self-discipline, resilience, and the pursuit of virtue. Written as a journal during his military campaigns, Meditations reveals Aurelius's attempts to navigate life's challenges with wisdom and inner strength.

The book centers on key Stoic ideas such as accepting what we cannot control, focusing on our responses, and cultivating virtues like humility, patience, and courage. Aurelius reminds readers to remain calm and rational, to act with purpose, and to avoid being swayed by fleeting desires or fears. His reflections on mortality, the impermanence of life, and the importance of living in accordance with one's values offer a grounded perspective on personal growth.

Meditations has resonated with readers for centuries because it presents profound insights in a straightforward, sincere style. It serves not only as a guide for those pursuing Stoic wisdom but also as an accessible source of advice on how to face life's uncertainties with integrity, clarity, and a focus on what truly matters.

Discipline is destiny by Ryan Holiday

Discipline Is Destiny by Ryan Holiday is a book that explores the importance of self-discipline as a foundation for personal and professional success. Part of his series on Stoic virtues, the book delves into how cultivating discipline can shape character, control impulses, and lead to a purposeful life.

Holiday emphasizes that true greatness and fulfillment come from consistent, deliberate choices rather than fleeting motivation or natural talent. He draws on examples from historical figures, athletes, leaders, and thinkers who used discipline to overcome adversity, achieve mastery, and leave a lasting impact.

The Power of your subconscious mind by Joseph Murphy

The Power of Your Subconscious Mind by Joseph Murphy is a profound exploration of the untapped potential within the subconscious mind. Murphy explains how our beliefs, thoughts, and mental patterns shape our experiences and reality. By understanding and reprogramming our subconscious, he argues, we can unlock a transformative power that influences our lives in profound ways—promoting healing, attracting success, and fostering personal growth.

About The Author

Ajaynath (Author)

Ajaynath is a Mechanical Engineer and Author from India. He hails from Thrissur, the cultural capital of Kerala, and his family home is in Chengaloor village.

He began his writing journey in short films and theatre before transitioning into philosophy, with a particular interest in Stoicism. His reflections and insights, initially shared through social media, became the driving force behind his writing career.

In addition to philosophy, he has a passion for videography, pencil drawing, and dogs. Currently, he resides in Al-Khobar, Saudi Arabia, where he works as a Procurement Engineer.

www.ingramcontent.com/pod-product-compliance
Lightning Source LLC
LaVergne TN
LVHW091538070526
838199LV00002B/116